Literature in Perspective

George Orw

B. T. Oxley

Evans

Evans Brothers Limited, London

Published by Evans Brothers Limited
Montague House, Russell Square, London, W.C.1

© B. T. Oxley 1967

First published 1967

Reprinted (with amendments) 1970
Reprinted (with revised Bibliography) 1973

Set in 11 on 12 point Bembo and printed offset in Great Britain by The Camelot Press Ltd, London and Southampton

Limp ISBN 0 237 44692 8

Cased ISBN 0 237 44691 X   PRA3187

Literature in Perspective

Of recent years, the ordinary man who reads for pleasure has been gradually excluded from that great debate in which every intelligent reader of the classics takes part. There are two reasons for this: first, so much criticism floods from the world's presses that no one but a scholar living entirely among books can hope to read it all; and second, the critics and analysts, mostly academics, use a language that only their fellows in the same discipline can understand.

Consequently criticism, which should be as 'inevitable as breathing'—an activity for which we are all qualified—has become the private field of a few warring factions who shout their unintelligible battle cries to each other but make little communication to the common man.

Literature in Perspective aims at giving a straightforward account of literature and of writers—straightforward both in content and in language. Critical jargon is as far as possible avoided; any terms that must be used are explained simply; and the constant preoccupation of the authors of the Series is to be lucid.

It is our hope that each book will be easily understood, that it will adequately describe its subject without pretentiousness so that the intelligent reader who wants to know about Donne or Keats or Shakespeare will find enough in it to bring him up to date on critical estimates.

Even those who are well read, we believe, can benefit from a lucid exposition of what they may have taken for granted, and perhaps—dare it be said?—not fully understood.

K. H. G.

George Orwell

I have used the following abbreviations of titles in the references. Unless otherwise stated below, the edition used is the uniform one published by Secker and Warburg. Where possible, however, I have also given a reference to a cheaper edition in paperbacks. Thus P is for Penguin, and COL E for *Collected Essays* in Mercury Paperbacks, published by Heinemann. In the references, only the page on which a quotation starts has been given. In some cases the quotations do extend over several pages of Orwell's text.

AF	Animal Farm
BD	Burmese Days
CD	A Clergyman's Daughter
CE	Critical Essays
CUA	Coming Up for Air
DOPL	Down and Out in Paris and London
EP	The English People (Collins)
EYE	England Your England
HC	Homage to Catalonia
KAF	Keep the Aspidistra Flying
LU	The Lion and the Unicorn
RWP	The Road to Wigan Pier
SE	Shooting an Elephant
1984	Nineteen Eighty-Four

When this book was first published, most of Orwell's journalism and correspondence was uncollected. There now exists the four-volume *Collected Essays, Journalism and Letters of George Orwell* (ed. S. Orwell and I. Angus, Secker and Warburg, 1968). It has not been possible to include any new material in the present reprint.

I should like to thank Kenneth Grose for his help (which has covered many things over many years) and comments.

B.T.O.

6

Contents

The Author

B. T. Oxley, M.A., Ph.D., is Lecturer in Literature at the University of Bradford.

Acknowledgements

The author and publishers are indebted to Paul Popper Ltd. for permission to reproduce the cover portrait; the Radio Times Hulton Picture Library for the photographs of the Jarrow Crusade and the man on a street corner; and the Imperial War Museum for the photographs of the German Labour Service marching before Hitler and the man in Belsen Concentration Camp.

They are also indebted to the estate of the late George Orwell, and Secker & Warburg, for permission to quote from the works of George Orwell, and to the following publishers and other copyright-holders for permission to use extracts from these books: *A Study of George Orwell* by Christopher Hollis (Hollis & Carter Ltd.); *Four Absentees* by R. Heppenstall (Barrie & Rockliff); *Dante Called You Beatrice* by P. Potts (Eyre & Spottiswoode Ltd.); *Salvaging of Civilization* by H. G. Wells (the Executor of H. G. Wells); *A Short History of the World* by H. G. Wells (Professor G. P. Wells, F.R.S.); *World Within World* by Stephen Spender (A. D. Peters & Co.); *How to Read* by Ezra Pound (Arthur V. Moore and New Directions Publishing Corporation and the Committee for Ezra Pound); *A Question of Upbringing* by Anthony Powell (William Heinemann Ltd. and Little, Brown & Company, Boston), and *Courage of Genius* by Robert Conquest (Collins). Also from these essays: 'On Roger Fry' from *Essays, Poems and Letters* by Julian Bell (The Hogarth Press); one by J. Symons in *The London Magazine* (Sept. 1963); the Introduction by Bertrand Russell to the June 1950 issue of *World Review* (Lord Russell) and an essay by Stephen Spender on *Homage to Catalonia* in the same issue (Stephen Spender).

Epigraph

Julian Bell, son of Vanessa and Clive Bell, nephew of Virginia Woolf, was killed driving an ambulance in the Battle of Brunete, outside Madrid, on 18th July 1937. Just over a year before that he had written these words:

> Like nearly all the intellectuals of this generation, we are fundamentally political in thought and action: this more than anything else marks the difference between us and our elders. Being socialist for us means being rationalist, common-sense, empirical; means a very firm extrovert, practical commonplace sense of exterior reality. It means turning away from mysticisms, fantasies, escapes into the inner life. We think of the world first and foremost as the place where other people live, as the scene of crisis and poverty, the probable scene of revolution and war: we think more about the practical solution of the real contradictions of the real world than possible discoveries in some other world.
>
> ON ROGER FRY, A Letter to A

This statement speaks nearly enough for Orwell—who was five years older than Bell—for it to stand as an epigraph to the following essay.

For
G
and
J, S & H

I

Writer, Man and Writing

DOCUMENTARY, PAMPHLET, POLEMIC

'In a peaceful age I might have written ornate or merely descriptive books, and might have remained almost unaware of my political loyalties. As it is I have been forced into becoming a sort of pamphleteer.'

George Orwell wrote that towards the end of his life in an essay called 'Why I Write' (1946), where he goes on to say:

> What I have most wanted to do throughout the past ten years is to make political writing into an art. My starting point is always a feeling of partisanship, a sense of injustice. When I sit down to write a book, I do not say to myself, 'I am going to produce a work of art'. I write it because there is some lie that I want to expose, some fact to which I want to draw attention, and my initial concern is to get a hearing. But I could not do the work of writing a book, or even a long magazine article, if it were not also an aesthetic experience. Anyone who cares to examine my work will see that even when it is downright propaganda it contains much that a full-time politician would consider irrelevant. EYE 13; COL E 424

Orwell classified anyone's motives for writing under four headings: egoism ('Desire to seem clever, to be talked about, to be remembered after death'); aesthetic enthusiasm ('Perception of beauty in the external world, or . . . in words and their right arrangement'); historical impulse ('Desire to see things as they are, to find out true facts and store them up for the use of posterity'); and political purpose ('Desire to push the world in a certain direction, to alter other people's idea of the kind of society that they should strive after').

In the essay just quoted he comments:

> I cannot say with certainty which of my motives are the strongest, but I know which of them deserve to be followed. And looking back through my work, I see that it is invariably where I lacked a *political* purpose that I wrote lifeless books and was betrayed into purple passages, sentences without meaning, decorative adjectives and humbug generally.   EYE 16; COL E 426

In one of his extremely helpful essays on Orwell (reprinted in *Essays on Literature and Ideas*, Macmillan, 1963) John Wain starts with the point that in approaching any author you must first decide what type of literature he is trying to write. This is what Renaissance critics were making possible when they established various genres of literature, each with its own aims, methods and conventions. Different kinds of writing would arouse different kinds of expectation in the reader, make different demands on him, call for some responses rather than others, possibly even call for differing scales of values. For example, if you try to read a play by Shakespeare with the expectations aroused by a modern prose play, you will make misjudgments far more easily than you will if you approach it with the expectations aroused by a medieval morality play.

H. G. Wells—one of the leading writers of Orwell's youth, and a very useful comparative figure—wrote in his *Experiment in Autobiography*: 'I refuse to play the "artist". .... I am a journalist all the time and what I write *goes* now—and will presently die.' There is much of this attitude, particularly its concern with the present (what 'goes now'), in Orwell. And unless you realize that his starting point is what he himself called historical impulse and political purpose you may find yourself wasting a good deal of time attacking him for not succeeding in doing something that he wasn't particularly concerned to do anyway.

It is clear that Orwell is not a literary figure in the way that—to use his own examples—Henry James or James Joyce were. He argued that such an 'aesthetic' attitude to life was impossible for anyone trying to account for the realities of the nineteen-thirties. It is difficult to imagine him producing the kind of elaborate, literary prose of James's later novels; it is impossible to imagine him spending, as Joyce did, nearly twenty years building up a complex verbal-structure like *Finnegans Wake*. Much of his work, in any case, is strictly non-literary (in the sense that it is non-imaginative—sociological or political analysis): *Down and Out in Paris and London*; *The Road to Wigan Pier*; *Homage to Catalonia*; *The Lion and the Unicorn*; the essays. Most of these last are admittedly about literary subjects, but usually take a more or less political direction rather than offer a technical analysis of the way a certain writer organizes words. It is indicative of a similar line of interest that, at least on the evidence of the work that is at present accessible, Orwell showed little concern with the pictorial arts, little with the dramatic and none at all with the musical.

There is a suggestion in *The Road to Wigan Pier* that at that time Orwell regarded himself as primarily a novelist. By 1937 he had published three novels and he declared: 'If I live to be sixty I shall probably have produced thirty novels, or enough to fill two medium-sized library shelves.' But a clearer view of his own abilities appears in a letter he wrote to his friend Julian Symons, who had raised a point about the difficulties of using a first-person narration as in *Coming Up for Air*: '. . . you are perfectly right about my own character constantly intruding on that of the narrator. I am not a real novelist anyway.' And many of his critics now agree with this verdict, arguing that the real backbone of his work is to be found in the essays—a form of writing mainly characterized by just such a personal intrusion on the part of the author.

Again, the nineteen-thirties generally was a time of considerable literary experimentation, but, as a novelist, Orwell showed little interest in moving out of the form as he found it in the novels he had read as a boy in Edwardian England. (The nearest he comes to a formal literary experiment is in the Trafalgar Square sequence in *A Clergyman's Daughter*.) Failure to experiment is, of course, no condemnation—Jane Austen similarly accepted the form she inherited—but it does perhaps suggest a lack of 'aesthetic' interest.

Nor, again as a novelist, could Orwell be considered as a 'poetic' writer—an inventor of symbols in the way that, for example, Dickens or Lawrence or William Golding is. When Orwell does use symbolism it tends to be in a rather obvious and mechanical way: the Italian militiaman he came across in Barcelona (see p. 70); Gordon Comstock's aspidistra in *Keep the Aspidistra Flying*; George Bowling's fishing in *Coming Up for Air*; the animals in *Animal Farm*; the room above the second-hand shop in *Nineteen Eighty-Four*. An attempt to explore these novels in terms of metaphor and imagery would probably be unrewarding compared with a similar analysis of, say, *Bleak House*, *Women in Love* or *Lord of the Flies*.

Orwell's prose is that of the journalist—and it is important to understand that there is nothing derogatory in that. But if you read aloud the following passage from a novel called *A Question of Upbringing* (chosen largely because I happen to have been reading it, but its author, Anthony Powell, knew Orwell and also went to Eton) you will get an idea of what Orwell's prose is very definitely *not* like:

> As winter advanced in that river valley, mist used to rise in late afternoon and spread over the flooded grass; until the house and all the outskirts of the town were enveloped in opaque, chilly vapour, tinted like cigar-smoke. The house looked on to other tenement-like structures, experiments in architectural insignificance, that intruded upon a central concentration of buildings, commanding and antiquated, laid out in a quadrilateral, though irregular, style. Silted-up residues of the years smouldered uninterruptedly—and not without melancholy—in the maroon brickwork of these medieval closes; beyond the cobbles and archways of which (in a more northerly direction) memory also brooded, no less enigmatic and inconsolable, among water-meadows and avenues of trees: the sombre demands of the past becoming at times almost suffocating in their insistence.

Such an urbane, sophisticated style, with its highly complex sentence structure, is quite foreign to Orwell (compare it for example with the passage quoted on p. 16). Again it is important to remember that 'simple' English is just as artificial, and as difficult to write well, as is the highly 'mannered' language of the above passage. There is as much literary skill involved in creating the slangy, colloquial vitality of *Coming Up for Air* as there is in Powell's prose.

Even in the obviously imaginative part of his work there are indications of a non-literary direction. In the first place, the novel is the least demanding of literary forms—it has a minimum of given structure, and its length allows a formal slackness impossible in other kinds of literary writing. Secondly, in its insistence on probability and particularity (it realistically describes actions performed by certain individuals at a certain time in a certain social situation), the novel is very close to the newspaper report. It is not an accident that novelists like Defoe, Fielding and Dickens were at one time—as was Orwell himself—professional journalists. The difficulty of classifying a book like *Down and Out in Paris and London* (which in its original Penguin edition of 1940 appeared as 'Fiction') is an indication of the kind of no-man's land that exists in this area.

Further, within this 'non-literary' context of the novel, you can see how Orwell's own stories suddenly stop being that, and start to become essays. Occasionally the shift is made obvious, as in the case of the pretended excerpts from 'The Theory and Practice of Oligarchical Collectivism' printed as part of *Nineteen Eighty-Four*. And you can hardly miss a similar change in the comments on private schools in *A Clergyman's Daughter*, or when Orwell takes over from Flory in the comments on imperialism in *Burmese Days*. The one novel (excluding *Animal Farm*, which is a special kind of story) where this is least obvious, I think—despite Orwell's own admission to Symons—is *Coming Up for Air*, where you are not so jolted by the change of view-point from protagonist's to author's because both can be contained in the 'I' who is the narrator.

From a purely literary point of view (and the whole point of much of Orwell's argument was to suggest that such a phrase was meaningless—see, for example, the remarks quoted in the second section of Chapter 6), it may be that his only complete success was *Animal Farm*. Here he found a metaphor which he could allow to speak for itself; and perhaps the shortness of the book has much to do with that.

It is interesting to look over Orwell's work as a whole and pick out what one regards as its best moments. For me, these would be: the description of the revolutionary excitement of the animals, and of the taking away of Boxer, in *Animal Farm*; the picture of Mrs. Creevy and her school in *A Clergyman's Daughter*; the revocation of pre-1914 Lower Binfield in *Coming Up for Air*; the account of the confrontation between Smith and O'Brien in the last section of *Nineteen Eighty-Four*. But just as much, I think of essays like 'A Hanging' or 'Shooting an Elephant'; of the analysis of boys' weekly comics and rude seaside postcards; of the passages describing the kitchens in Paris and the spikes in the Home Counties (*Down and Out in Paris and London*), the Brookers' lodging house, the coal-face and its workers (*The Road to Wigan Pier*), the front line in Aragon (*Homage to Catalonia*). This sort of thing:

> Except for about an hour, I was at work from seven in the morning till a quarter past nine at night; first at washing crockery, then at scrubbing the tables and floors of the employees' dining-room, then at polishing glasses and knives, then at fetching meals, then at washing crockery again, then at fetching more meals and washing more crockery. It was easy work, and I got on well with it except when I went to the kitchen to fetch meals. The kitchen was like nothing I had ever seen or imagined—a stifling, low-ceilinged inferno of a cellar, red-lit from the fires, and deafening with oaths and the clanging of pots and pans. It was so hot that all the metal-work except the stoves had to be covered with cloth. In the middle were furnaces, where twelve cooks skipped to and fro, their faces dripping sweat in spite of their white caps. Round that were counters where a mob of waiters and *plongeurs* clamoured with trays. Scullions, naked to the waist, were stoking the fires and scouring huge copper saucepans with sand. Everyone seemed to be in a hurry and a rage. The head cook, a fine, scarlet man with big moustachios, stood in the middle booming continuously, '*Ça marche deux œufs brouillés! Ça marche un Chateaubriand aux pommes sautées!*' except when he broke off to curse at a *plongeur*.

DOPL 57; P 51

Orwell's strength is in this kind of 'reportage'—a word which implies something less ephemeral than ordinary journalism, yet something less elaborate than sociology. One other word for such writing (suggested by John Mander in his book *The Writer and Commitment*, Secker, 1961) is 'documentary'. And this is a term particularly associated with the nineteen-thirties during which Orwell mainly developed into what he was—for example, in the film industry or in the publications of an organization set up in 1937 and known as Mass Observation. There is a long tradition of 'documentary' writing in English letters—works like Defoe's *A Journal of the Plague Year*, Mayhew's *London Labour and the London Poor*, Jack London's *The People of the Abyss* —and much of Orwell's work, both fictional and non-fictional, fits neatly into it.

'Documentary' is different from sociology in that it is more personal, more impressionist, more concerned to recreate the experience of an atmosphere than to communicate or classify a mass of carefully collected detail. Those who don't like the form—often those trained in academic sociology—suggest that it is the amateur's corruption of the real thing, that it is dangerous because it thrives on impossible generalization and prejudices pretending to be facts. This may be true; but, in any case, this is a form to which, since Orwell's death, we have become very much accustomed on television—not so much in the form of on-the-spot news reports, as in that of the more extended programmes of men like Malcolm Muggeridge or Alan Whicker.

Orwell himself, as in the quotation which opened this chapter, described his activity as that of the pamphleteer (he was interested in the form, and wrote an introduction to a collection of English examples). The pamphleteer is a man writing very much from a certain position—usually a political one—trying to argue his reader into seeing what the author himself regards as the truth. And Orwell was very much concerned with the problems facing the writer-as-pamphleteer (see Chapter 6). Those who feel that the argument is too unfair, that they are being bullied or tricked rather than reasoned with, substitute for 'pamphlet' the word 'polemic'—which at least allows the reader to see in some sort of excusing context Orwell's notorious and otherwise damaging fondness for unfounded generalization, for assertion instead of argument, for occasional silliness, for such minor tricks as the emotional and deprecatory use of 'little' (these are all analysed by Raymond Williams in *Culture and Society*, Penguin, 1961). If you feel hostile to Orwell to start with, you will find in his work plenty of material to keep you on the boil.

Orwell has sometimes been described as the Jeremiah of the thirties, sometimes as the Lollard of Social Democracy (the Lollards were 14th-century English heretics who rebelled against what they considered to be the corrupt practice of the Roman Catholic Church), but most often he has been seen as 'the conscience of the Left'—as a man who spent much of his life pointing out to radical socialists that in their fight against West European Fascism they ran the danger of making themselves blind to that other form of totalitarianism known as Stalinism.

Sir Richard Rees, who knew Orwell for nearly twenty years and who is his literary executor, sees him as a writer of protest coming chronologically between H. G. Wells (before the First World War) and John Osborne (after the Second). His own book on Orwell is subtitled 'Fugitive from the Camp of Victory' and this phrase (itself taken from a book by Simone Weil) pinpoints rather well a central aspect of this writer's life and work (see the first section of Chapter 3).

Orwell himself once wrote a description of how he imagined Dickens to appear.

> It is the face of a man who is always fighting against something, but who fights in the open and is not frightened, the face of a man who is *generously angry*—in other words, of a nineteenth-century liberal, a free intelligence, a type hated . . . by all the smelly little orthodoxies which are now contending for our souls.
>
> CE 59; COL E 87

Fighting and not being frightened; angry (though not always so generously as the 19th-century liberal could afford to be); the free intelligence hated by 20th-century orthodoxy—there is,

18

not surprisingly, as much of Orwell as there is of Dickens in the portrait.

ERIC BLAIR

The writer whose real name was Blair asked that no biography of him should be written, and until very recently that wish has been respected. The fact that he wrote under a pen-name may partly suggest that he wished to keep separate his personal life as a man and his more public life as a writer of political polemics. But several of his friends have left scattered reminiscences of the private man, some of which contain hints that help to explain features of the writing.

Cyril Connolly knew Orwell for a longer period than almost anyone else (although they lost touch with one another between 1922 and 1934). In his book, *Enemies of Promise* (Penguin, 1961), there is this recollection of their prep. school days (St. Wulfric's is not its real name):

> I was a stage rebel, Orwell a true one. . . . The remarkable thing about Orwell was that alone among the boys he was an intellectual and not a parrot for he thought for himself, read Shaw and Samuel Butler and rejected not only St. Wulfric's, but the war, the Empire, Kipling, Sussex, and Character. 178

Christopher Hollis, a fellow Etonian, tells a story in *A Study of George Orwell* (Hollis and Carter, 1956) of how a sixth-former, believing himself to be cheeked by one of Orwell's year over the borrowing of some tennis balls, arranged for all the boys to be beaten:

> There was a tremendous argument whether they had insulted him or not, and in that argument Orwell stood out as the spokesman for his Election—first, maintaining that there had been no insult and then, with melodramatic gesture, that at least there could be no point in beating the whole Election. It would suffice if there was a scapegoat and for that he offered himself. The argument was to no purpose, and the whole Election was beaten. . . . It certainly was not true that he was unpopular with his fellow Collegers. It certainly was not true that he was insignificant among them or what I might

call superficially solitary. . . . Anarchical opinions by no means made Orwell isolated. They made him a notable leader. They put him in the fashion. . . . Perhaps there was in his rebellion a kind of obstinate and puritan sincerity which contrasted a little with the more light-hearted ragging in which at any rate the greater number of the escapades of the rest of us were conceived. . . . There was a custom at Eton by which boys touched their caps to a master when they passed him. It seemed, and seems to me, a very harmless courtesy and, questioning all else, I had never thought to question that custom, but I remember discovering to my surprise that Orwell resented passionately the indignity of this servile action that was demanded of him.   15-17

(Connolly, speaking of the Eton days, describes Orwell as perpetually sneering at 'They'—'a sort of Marxist-Shavian concept which included Masters, old Collegers, the Church and Senior reactionaries'.)

Stephen Spender, who seems to have met Orwell in 1938 when they had a common interest in the course of the Spanish Civil War, also discusses this Etonian background in an article on *Homage to Catalonia* published in *World Review* (June 1950):

Orwell was *really* what hundreds of others only pretend to be. He was really classless, really a Socialist, really truthful. The rule of his authenticity is made clear perhaps by the exceptional thing which might make him appear to be an upper-class moral adventurer who had neurotically strayed into the camp of the opposing class: the fact that he was an Etonian. For his Eton background was utterly irrelevant. He was what he was simply out of good faith and honesty, not out of neurosis or ecstasy or a sense of mystery. He was perhaps the least Etonian character who has ever come from Eton. He was a tall, lean, scraggy man, a Public House character, with a special gleam in his eye, and a home-made way of arguing from simple premises, which could sometimes lead him to radiant common sense, sometimes to crankiness.

Julian Symons became friends with Orwell during the Second World War (the two of them apparently had a weekly lunch with Anthony Powell and Malcolm Muggeridge). He makes the point—here taken up at the beginning of Chapter 3 and at the end of Chapter 5—about Orwell as an outsider and victim almost inviting the 'assaults of life' (his article is reprinted in *Critical Occasions*, Hamish Hamilton, 1966):

> From the beginning of his adult life Orwell was a man struggling against the neuroses implanted in him by his birth and childhood. He was ugly, he was awkward—or at least he thought so—and he was poor. These things made him an outcast, and suspicious. A vital . . . moment in his life was that when outcast Blair, the unsuccessful writer, took on a new skin and became George Orwell. For some time the new skin didn't fit well, the old Blair kept peeping out of it, but . . . [his letters] show a man growing positively wiser, more humane, more tolerant. He was helped in this by literary success, but he developed also, it seems to me, through a conscious effort of the will. People rarely improve as they grow older, but Orwell did. Even in my six years' knowledge of him he became what I can only describe as a better man. . . . Finally his unique merit rested in the fact that, unlike most people, he always welcomed and even invited the assaults of life. . . . He opposed with all the force of his nature the orthodoxies of his time, Stalinism and bureaucratic Socialism to which almost all Left wing or Liberal intellectuals adhered. When one looks at him from a distance mistakes and contradictions melt away, leaving the image of an admirable human being, one who looked deliberately at the worst horrors of his time with a gaze direct, generous and unafraid.
>
> 204–5

Rayner Heppenstall shared a flat with Orwell during the mid-thirties (and was once, coming home drunk, knocked down by him). The following recollection—from *Four Absentees* (Barrie and Rockliff, 1960)—is ostensibly of about 1935, but is obviously coloured by a later knowledge of Orwell:

> I shall not much exaggerate if I say that both Michael and I regarded Eric as a nice old thing, a kindly eccentric. We liked him, but we did not always take him seriously. For my own part, I even tended to exploit him a little. . . . To us, indeed, he seemed ill-read. In the worst possible sense, we were both very highbrow. The kind of novel Eric wrote seemed to us not worth writing. . . . To us, Eric's tastes were peculiar. We did not really care for Samuel Butler, though Henry Miller was not bad, we supposed. I had assiduously read *The Magnet* until twelve years ago, and at Blackpool long

ago I had been amused by the picture-postcards, but I thought it odd to make a cult of these things in adult life. It did not seem to me to matter very much whether Edgar Wallace was a Fascist or not, since I was not tempted to read his books. . . . To us it was a curious mind, satirically attached to everything traditionally English, always full of interesting and out-of-the-way information like *Tit-Bits*, but arid, colourless, devoid of poetry, derisive, yet darkly obsessed. There underlay it all some unsolved equation of love and hate, some memory of childhood nursed through Eton, through Burma, taken out and viewed secretly in Paris kitchens or upon the thresholds of doss-houses. The fondness for country parsonages, comic postcards, *The Magnet* and *The Gem*, anecdotes about Queen Victoria and bishops, all betrayed something quite inaccessible to us.   59–63

Paul Potts is a poet who came to know Orwell during the final years. In *Dante Called You Beatrice* (Eyre and Spottiswoode, 1960), he describes a man he found 'Britishly balanced and Saxonly sane':

. . . there was something about him, the proud man apart, the Don Quixote on a bicycle . . . that caught one's imagination right away. That made one think of a knight errant and of social justice as the Holy Grail. One felt safe with him; he was so intellectually honest. His mind was a court where the judge was the lawyer for the defence. . . . He was proud and his pride got him into the literature of the world; he was chivalrous and his chivalry put him among the great radicals of England. . . . His mind was limited but he knew his own limitations. Inside those wide limits it was a first-rate mind. It had more kindness than love, but more anger than contempt. It was like a breath of fresh air to hear him talk about literature, politics, history or Victoriana. He was a storehouse of odd information about weird subjects. . . . he never joined a committee. He was once tempted to do so, he said, just so that he could resign. . . . He used words in fact to puncture the greed he did not share, and to call attention to a beauty he did not make. Freedom was a verb to him, equality a necessity. . . . I suppose what made Orwell so permanently attractive as a person, and so readable as a writer, was that he was so ordinary really, normal if not average. He had none of the extravagances of an artist, none of the irresponsibilities of a Bohemian, and none of the selfishness of an intellectual. He was Britishly balanced and Saxonly sane. . . . In short his life was a

duel fought against lies; the weapon he chose, the English language.
72–86

After he had been seriously wounded in Spain, Orwell wrote to Heppenstall:

> I am rather glad to have been hit by a bullet because I think it will happen to us all in the near future, and I am glad to know that it doesn't hurt to speak of.

How much Orwell had to be hurt before it was worth speaking of is not known, and before he died he had imagined a worse fate for humanity than being shot in the throat. But the first half of the sentence seems to typify the Fugitive from Victory, a man the present book tries to see as the propagandist of those victims of the 20th century with whom he felt a need to associate himself.

THE WORK

George Orwell's writing life lasted less than twenty years. His first essay was published in 1931, and his first book in 1933; he was writing his last book at the end of the forties.

This life-work can be seen as comprising fifteen books. These can be treated item by item, chronologically and in relation to the sort of background sketched in the next chapter. However, for the purposes of this book I have adopted another classification.

There are nine works of non-fiction (including two posthumous collections of essays):

Down and Out in Paris and London	1933
The Road to Wigan Pier	1937
Homage to Catalonia	1938
Inside the Whale	1940
The Lion and the Unicorn	1941
Critical Essays	1946
The English People	1947
Shooting an Elephant	1950
England Your England	1953

In addition there is a considerable amount of what might be called bread-and-butter work: contributions to various symposia, introductions, journalism like the weekly articles in *Tribune*, the regular reports to the American *Partisan Review*, occasional articles in *The Observer*. Much of this (as well as the essay 'Such, Such Were the Joys', Orwell's description of his prep-school which was for a long time considered too libellous for publication in England) is now in the four-volume *Collected Essays, Journalism and Letters*.

There are six works of fiction:

Burmese Days	1934
A Clergyman's Daughter	1935
Keep the Aspidistra Flying	1936
Coming Up for Air	1939
Animal Farm	1945
Nineteen Eighty-Four	1949

In the following presentation of Orwell's work, Chapter 2 offers a view of the public events of his half-century, regarded above all as a time of crisis and dislocation; Chapter 3 describes what seem to be Orwell's main themes, and draws on his non-fiction; Chapter 4 uses *Homage to Catalonia* and *Animal Farm* as epitomes of the evidence offered in the previous chapters; Chapter 5 tries to see the four conventional novels and *Nineteen Eighty-Four* as a homogeneous group, largely by tracing the fortunes of their various protagonists; Chapter 6 deals—in more detail than would have been possible had it been, logically, included as part of Chapter 3—with Orwell's concern with language and the position of the writer: perhaps the last and most central of all his heroes.

2

Orwell's Public World

The volume of *The New Cambridge Modern History* which covers the years 1898–1945 (nearly enough Orwell's own dates) is entitled 'The Era of Violence'. Its editor sees the period in terms of a blossoming of the seeds of violence and dehumanization scattered in the 19th century—a blossoming which showed the following main characteristics.

There was a tremendous technological and scientific advance, increasing the pace of industrialization and the numbers of town-dwellers. There was a growing belief in the necessity of long-term economic planning. There was the early spreading and, after 1918, rapid withering away, of democratic values and such structures as labour organizations or parliamentary socialist parties associated with the search for social justice. There was the rise of the revolutionary movements of Fascism and Communism leading to what they called, according to their various jargons, the corporative state, the *Reich* of a purified *Volk*, or the monolithic one-party state.

The half-century witnessed a chain of crises with their constant repercussions of instability and dislocation. Through these was shown the hopelessness of the general English assumption of 1900 that the future lay with parliamentary institutions—a hopelessness hammered home in the late thirties when the League of Nations collapsed through the failure of its attempts to stop some of the most savage reversals of civilized values ever known. Within thirty years there were two major wars separated by an economic disaster. In country after country the Rule of Law was replaced by that of the Leader, or of his torture chambers, concentration camps, mass propaganda and carefully drilled youth movements. Ironically the half-century also saw that at its end most Europeans were far more materially comfortable than they or their counterparts had been at its beginning.

Orwell was born in 1903. Thus at the outbreak of the First World War he was a boy of eleven, a pupil at a snobbish prep. school in the south of England, being trained for scholarship success. In 1917, when Lenin and the Bolsheviks forced the Russian Revolution away from any possibility of democratic government, he was in his first year at Eton. In 1922, when the League of Nations was dealing with its first problems, when Stalin became General Secretary of the Russian Communist Party and Mussolini became dictator of Italy, he was on the verge of adult life and a five-year career in the Indian Imperial Police.

In 1929, when the collapse of the New York Stock Exchange began the Depression, he was twenty-six, having worked off and on in various Parisian restaurants and lived with the down-and-outs of London. Behind him was the decision not to return to a colonialism that had come to seem outrageous. In 1933, when Hitler became Chancellor of a Germany with six million unemployed, when Stalin had just completed the first and most bloody stage of Russia's industrialization, he was thirty. He had worked as a teacher in a private school, and as a part-time assistant in a bookshop; he was preparing for the press his first book—*Down and Out in Paris and London*. In 1936, when the Spanish Civil War started, he was keeping a village store and had published three more books—his first novels. By now he was a man of sufficient literary repute (at least with his publisher, Gollancz) to be commissioned to write a book on the condition of the unemployed in Lancashire and Yorkshire.

By 1939 and the start of the Second World War he was married, and had gained in Spain his first-hand experience of modern war, and of the political persecution that seemed to be an inherent part of Stalin's Communism. When the hot war stopped and the cold one between Russia and the N.A.T.O. powers started in 1945-7, he was in his early forties. He had worked in the Eastern Section of the B.B.C., served in the Home

Guard, acted as literary editor of a left-wing weekly called *Tribune* and as a correspondent for *The Observer*. He was consumptive, widowed and left to look after a newly-adopted baby, trying to live during the summer months on an extremely isolated farm in the Hebrides. He was famous and, for the first time in his life, prosperous as the author of *Animal Farm*. When he died at the beginning of 1950 he was forty-six. He had driven himself through the last years of illness in order to finish *Nineteen Eighty-Four*—his final comment on an era of violence which in only two more years was going to possess thermo-nuclear 'devices', and which has moved ever since from one crisis to another.

THE BOYHOOD WORLD (1903–22)

Orwell's early boyhood was lived in that pre-war England which is called (historically speaking, rather inaccurately) Edwardian. It is an age which it is difficult not to see as a kind of Indian summer of European civilization. It was, for example, a time in which it was still possible to think in terms of 'progress'. At the beginning of his autobiography, *World Within World*, Stephen Spender describes the atmosphere of life on what he calls a 'liberal promontory of time' to which all other periods seemed gradually and improvingly to have led:

> If the history books were illustrated, they gave the impression that the world had been moving steadily forward in the past thousands of years, from the vague to the defined, the savage to the civilized, the crude to the scientific, the unfamiliar to the known. It was as though the nineteenth century had been a machine absorbing into itself at one end humanity dressed in fancy dress, unwashed, fierce and immoral, and emitting at the other modern men in their utilitarian clothes with their hygienic houses, their zeal for reform, their air of having triumphed by mechanical, economic and scientific means over the passionate, superstitious, cruel and poetic past.

The First World War did much to destroy this belief. In 1921, H. G. Wells published *The Salvaging of Civilization*, where he wrote:

A series of immense and tragic events have shattered the self-complacency and challenged the will and intelligence of mankind. That easy general forward movement of human affairs which for several generations had seemed to justify the persuasion of a necessary and invincible progress, progress towards greater powers, greater happiness, and a continual enlargement of life, has been checked violently and perhaps arrested altogether. The spectacular catastrophe of the great war has revealed an accumulation of destructive forces in our outwardly prosperous society, of which few of us had dreamt; and it has also revealed a profound incapacity to deal with and restrain these forces.

Yet the strength of the persuasion of invincible progress is suggested by the fact that in the very next year Wells published *A Short History of the World*—one of the most popular history books of the half-century—which ends on this famous note:

Man is still only adolescent. His troubles are not the troubles of senility and exhaustion but of increasing and still undisciplined strength. When we look at all history as one process... when we see the steadfast upward struggle of life towards vision and control, then we see in their true proportions the hopes and dangers of the present time. As yet we are hardly in the earliest dawn of human greatness. . . . Can we doubt that presently our race will more than realise our boldest imaginations, that it will achieve unity and peace, that it will live, the children of our blood and lives will live, in a world made more splendid and lovely than any palace or garden that we know, going on from strength to strength in an ever-widening circle of adventure and achievement? What man has done, the little triumphs of his present state, and all this history we have told, form but the prelude to the things that man has yet to do.

Such an attitude is foreign to us; it was foreign to the writers of the thirties who were more or less Orwell's contemporaries; how foreign it was to Orwell himself can be seen by comparing Wells's second statement with those quoted at the beginning of Chapter 3. (In fairness it must be said that it was again foreign to Wells after 1939. His last book, published in 1945, was called *Mind at the End of Its Tether*.)

Edwardian England, built on the foundation of what is sometimes called the Great Peace of 1815–1914, was a liberal-capitalist society. It was the most highly industrialized region of the world; it was the centre of an Empire covering one quarter of the world's surface, containing one quarter of its population, and owning one half of its merchant-shipping tonnage. Largely on the basis of naval power, Great Britain was a world force; largely on the basis of the strength of sterling, London was the centre of world finance, insurance and investment.

Internally such a society was in many ways an unjust one. The distribution of wealth is said to have been about as unequal as it has ever been, and the main social fact of the time (it is still present in the society described in *The Road to Wigan Pier* which was published in 1937) was the clear rift between the eighty per cent working class and the rest. This is the last period of English history in which domestic servants figure as a considerable social group. But it is also the first period in which poverty came to be studied seriously and regarded as something remediable, just as it is the first to worry itself about the problem of chronic mass-unemployment. (The results of Rowntree's investigations into poverty in York were published in 1901; Jack London's much less academic *The People of the Abyss* appeared in 1903; William Beveridge's *Unemployment, a Problem of Industry* and C. F. G. Masterman's *The Condition of England* both appeared in 1909.)

In 1914 Beatrice Webb—she and her husband were the leading socialist intellectuals of the time—noted in her diary that 'the landslide in England towards Social Democracy proceeds steadily'. The landslide has ended in what we call the cradle-to-grave welfare state, and in what sociologists call the 'bourgeoisification of the class structure', by which they mean that we are now all members of one wide middle class rather than of one of those sub-divisions that Orwell himself liked to manipulate.

The pre-1914 aspects of the slide—tremendously accelerated by the impact of the First World War during which, for example, several major industries were virtually nationalized—were threefold: the beginnings of government-directed social security (technically known as 'collectivism'), of full parliamentary democracy, and of a much more open system of secondary and further education. But the social democratic landslide also contained other premonitions. The same pre-war years saw the growth of a belief in 'direct action' rather than in parliamentary processes: the idea of a general strike, the work of a militant suffragette movement, the Irish nationalism which came to its climax in the Easter Rising of 1916.

If the time of Orwell's childhood seems impossibly remote, remember that the period produced Einstein's work on relativity, Thomson's in nuclear physics, Rutherford's in radio-activity, Bragg's in X-ray crystallography. It saw the arrival of the motor car as something more than an eccentricity, of the aeroplane, of wireless telegraphy (the broadcasting of speech and music was a later development), of the cinema, of mass-literacy. These years saw the publication of major works by Hardy, James and Conrad, by Yeats, Bennett, Galsworthy and H. G. Wells, by Shaw, Kipling and Forster; but they also saw the publication of the first three novels of D. H. Lawrence and of the early work of Pound and Joyce. Those who listened to the new works of Elgar and Delius could also have seen the Russian Ballet dancing to the music of Stravinsky; those who went to see paintings by Sargent and Orpen could also have gone to the 1910 Post-Impressionist Exhibition or to the first London showing of Picasso.

On the evidence of his published work, music and art appear to have meant little to Orwell, but he seems to have been very familiar with many of the writers of this time. In *The Road to Wigan Pier* he refers to himself as an eighteen-year-old snob who had 'read and re-read the entire published works of Shaw, Wells and Galsworthy (at that time still regarded as dangerously "advanced" writers)'. Cyril Connolly describes him as a schoolboy immersed in Butler's *The Way of All Flesh*—published in 1903, this novel seems to have brought to many of its readers a liberation from what we would call 'Victorianism'—and in the 'atheistic arguments' of Shaw's *Androcles and the Lion*. It is a mistake, of course, to allow Orwell's early reading of Edwardian literature a disproportionate influence. As an adult he seems to have felt the greatest affinity with Swift, Dickens and George Gissing—and only the last can be squeezed into the period now being discussed.

Orwell was too young to have immediate experience of the First World War which brought Edwardian England to an end, and much of what we recognize as War Literature, through which he might have obtained a second-hand experience of that episode, was not in fact created until considerably later—when it played its part in the pacifist movements of the early thirties. Yet the war is important in any consideration of his life and times insofar as it was a symbol of barbarism's first major assault on modern European civilization, and insofar as it was the seed-bed of so many of the crises which are to be described in the rest of this chapter. Thus out of the chaos of the Russian military defeats of 1916 and 1917 came the Revolution which many think is the central event of the half-century, and out of that came Stalinism. Out of the Versailles peace terms and the demand for reparations came the economic disintegration of the Weimar Republic; out of that came the National Socialist German Workers' Party, which was founded in 1919, and out of that came Hitler. Out of the post-war unrest in Italy came the King's fear of a Communist rising, and out of that fear came Mussolini's Fascism.

England escaped these extremes, just as she had escaped much of the physical destruction caused by the war, but the immediate post-war years produced two areas of serious trouble. There was a growing bitterness in industrial relations (particularly in the coal industry which Orwell was to describe fifteen years later), and this almost led to a general strike in 1921 when there were over two million unemployed. There was also the brutal suppression between 1920 and 1922 of a further Irish nationalist rebellion by those auxiliary units of the Irish Constabulary known as the Black and Tans.

Most of Orwell's time at Eton was passed in these years which seem to offer little support to President Wilson's contention, expressed in a speech in Manchester at the end of 1918, that men were beginning to see 'not perhaps the golden age, but an age which at any rate is brightening from decade to decade'. One reason for optimism might have been the founding of the League of Nations—but within fifteen years that experiment was to collapse. In the light of the course Orwell's career was to follow, those who like finding symbols may take pleasure in the fact that 1922, the year in which he left England, was also the year in which T. S. Eliot published *The Waste Land*.

THE ADULT WORLD (1—1922–39)

Orwell left his own country to go to a part of the world which looked as if it was going to experience the troubles characteristic of Ireland. India and Burma were still feeling the repercussions of what is known as the Amritsar Massacre of 1919 when a General Dyer, firing without warning on demonstrating Punjabi Indians, killed 379 and wounded 1,200 of them. Anti-colonialist nationalism was fermented by the First World War just as it was by the Second. Gandhi became leader of the Indian National Congress Party in 1917; his first major campaign of non-co-operation and civil disobedience was in 1920–1, and he was imprisoned for the first time by the British in 1922. In Burma itself (where Orwell was actually to work, but which was administered as part of India until 1937) there was a flare up of nationalism in 1921 when it became clear that the country was not to be included in the reforms offered to India.

For the first five years of his adult life Orwell was relatively isolated from European affairs. But what he experienced as an official administering the colonialist expansion of Europe into Asia (and the Burmese reaction to that extension is suggested by the fact that in 1942 they welcomed the Japanese invaders as liberators), influenced his response to the western civilization to which he returned. This civilization he saw as a struggle between the oppressors and the oppressed—and it was a struggle which he witnessed, wrote about and joined for the remaining twenty-odd years of his life.

The England to which Orwell came back in 1927 was a country suffering from what has been called 'capitalism-in-decay'. A song at the end of the First World War had asked 'What shall we be when we aren't what we are?' and the answer for many turned out to be 'The unemployed'. In fact between 1922 and 1940 the unemployment figures never

32

dropped below one million, and the presence of these men seemed to many to prove the Marxist view of the essential degeneracy of capitalism. The class bitterness still hanging in the air from the 1926 General Strike, and from the much longer coal strike, was exacerbated by the coming of the Depression and the economies in the social services brought about by the financial crisis of 1931. Any account of the early thirties, when Orwell, living on his leave pay, was trying to establish himself as a writer, will use again and again its familiar vocabulary: dole, depressed areas, malnutrition, slum, public assistance committee, means-test. All this is symbolized by the plight of one town in the north-east—Jarrow, where in 1935 nearly three-quarters of all insured workers were out of work. It was from this place, which came to be known as 'the town they killed', that there set out the most famous of the many protest marches of the time.

The main visual images of these years are those of derelict dockyards, lines of back-to-back houses, and men waiting for nothing at the street corners of mining towns where there was no work. It is the scenery of some of W. H. Auden's early poetry, of Walter Greenwood's novel *Love on the Dole* (1933), of the second half of J. B. Priestley's *English Journey* (1934), or of the first part of Orwell's own *The Road to Wigan Pier* (1937).

From this state of capitalism-in-decay sprang three features of the thirties in England with which Orwell was mainly concerned: the growth of the British Labour Party to replace Liberalism as the main force of democratic opposition; the growth and tactics of the Communist Party of Great Britain (C.P.G.B.), particularly insofar as these were symptomatic of Russian Stalinism; and the growth of British Fascism, again particularly insofar as it was symptomatic of certain continental developments.

The British Labour Party provided a very brief minority government in 1924, and another slightly more lasting one in 1929–31, when for the first time it was the largest single party in the Commons, though still without an over-all majority. In 1918 it had adopted a constitution containing the Clause Four which was to become notorious in Party Conference debates forty years later, and which defined the Socialist aims of the party:

> To secure for the producers by hand or by brain the full fruits of their industry, and the most equitable distribution thereof that may be possible, upon the basis of the common ownership of the means of production and the best obtainable system of popular administration and control of each industry or service.

In 1928 the Party adopted a new programme, denying that it had any 'sentimental aspiration for an impossible Utopia' or that it was merely 'a blind movement against poverty and oppression':

> It is a conscious, systematic and unflagging effort to use the weapons forged in the victorious struggle for political democracy to end the capitalist dictatorship in which democracy finds everywhere its most insidious and most relentless foe.

Orwell also wanted to end a capitalist dictatorship which seemed to him to degrade human life as much as colonialism did. But he wanted to be sure that the weapons forged in the struggle for democracy were in better hands than those of many of the members of the Labour Party as he saw them in the mid-thirties. And he wanted to be certain that other forms of dictatorship should be recognized as possibly more insidious and certainly more relentless than the traditional one. After 1935–6 it became clear to him that the nature of the dictatorship was in fact altering. This alteration corresponds to a shift in interest from home affairs to one in foreign affairs. (As far as I know, the major internal crisis of the time—the abdication of Edward VIII in December 1936—is unnoticed by Orwell, who at the time was on his way to Spain.) Appeasement, re-armament, collective security through the League of Nations, economic sanctions against aggressors—these are the phrases of the second half of the thirties that replace the vocabulary of the Depression—just as Addis Ababa, Madrid, Munich and Prague seemed to be the places where things were happening, rather than Jarrow and the mining towns of South Wales.

Foreign affairs for Orwell at this time meant the contemporary history of Spain, Russia and Germany. His reaction to events in the first two countries is discussed in Chapter 4; here can be mentioned the two English movements which reflected some of this contemporary European history.

The British Communist Party was founded in 1920. During the thirties its membership increased from just over 2,500 to nearly 18,000, and the peak was reached in 1942 after Hitler's invasion of Russia when there were 56,000 members. Despite references to the Marxist mood of a pink decade, it is clear that the Party, compared for example with the very strong French, German and Italian Parties, has never been a considerable factor in British politics. Throughout the period only a handful of men has ever represented it in parliament, and its election record has been generally disastrous. This failure has been attributed to the fact that the Party was a revolutionary group having to work in a non-revolutionary situation. The frustration of this position was increased by what is known as the 'bolshevization' of the Party, completed by 1929, which entailed its complete subservience to a tactical line formulated in Moscow. The necessary adherence to this line produced that intellectual flexibility (Orwell was eventually to christen it 'doublethink') by which, for example, what had been defined as a struggle against Fascism could become an imperialist war (after the signing of the Nazi-Soviet Pact in 1939), and could again become a struggle against Fascism (after the German attack on Russia in 1941).

English Socialism—and Orwell is part of its tradition—has always thought of itself as the descendant of Robert Owen and brotherly love rather than of Karl Marx and class war. (The first volume of *Das Kapital* was not translated into English until almost twenty years after its first appearance; and in fact the British Labour Party consistently refused to admit the C.P.G.B. as an affiliated body.)

The Communist Party was most important as an emotional force, a focal point of protest against unemployment and against Fascism, and relationship with it did not have to be defined too closely. Orwell himself once argued that the main stream of

35

English literature in the mid-thirties was virtually under Communist control; yet very few of the writers one thinks of in this context—for example, those who contributed to the early numbers of John Lehmann's anthology *New Writing* which started in 1936—were actual Party members.

There were two aspects of Communist Party activity in Britain. First there was its work in the formation of that alliance with other political groups (previously bitterly attacked but now to be wooed as anti-Fascist allies) which came to be known as the Popular Front. At a meeting of the Communist International in Moscow in 1935, its General Secretary had declared:

> The formation of a joint People's Front providing for joint action with Social Democratic parties is a necessity. Cannot we endeavour to unite the Communist, Social Democratic, Catholic and other workers? Comrades, you will remember the ancient tale of the capture of Troy. The attacking army was unable to achieve victory until, with the aid of the Trojan Horse, it penetrated to the very heart of the enemy camp. We, revolutionary workers, should not be shy of using the same tactics.

Spain and France saw the election of Popular Front governments, but in England the main manifestation of the movement was the formation of the Left Book Club in 1936. This organization, run by Victor Gollancz, Harold Laski and John Strachey (at this time one of the leading English Marxist theoreticians, whose most influential book *The Coming Struggle For Power* was published in 1932), issued monthly anti-Fascist books and set up discussion groups throughout the country. By the end of 1937 there were 50,000 members, and one of the publications they received (with some reluctance on Gollancz's part) was *The Road to Wigan Pier*, the first of Orwell's books to reach anything like a mass public.

The second aspect of Communist activity in England was its work in recruiting members of the International Brigade which was fighting in the Spanish Civil War against General Franco's right-wing military insurrection.

Above all, the C.P.G.B. was the English representative of a foreign totalitarian system known as Stalinism. This system was exemplified, for those of Orwell's time who did not regard it as the greatest social experiment ever undertaken, by the first two Five Year Plans (1928–37), which collectivized and starved out millions of Russian peasants, as well as building Russia into a 20th-century industrial power; by internal upheavals such as the Purge Trials (1936–8); and by foreign policy reversals such as the non-aggression pact with Germany (1939). To Orwell's own disgust such, to him, criminal activity could be conveniently forgotten when Stalin became a glorious ally in 1941. He noted in his diary for July of that year: 'I could not have a better example of the moral and emotional shallowness of our time, than the fact that we are now all more or less pro-Stalin. This disgusting murderer is temporarily on our side, and so the purges, etc., are suddenly forgotten.' It was because Orwell could not forget, and could not accept Stalinist Communism as a possible remedy for the chaotic suffering of capitalism-in-decay, that he is now frequently referred to as 'the conscience of the Left'.

Even more clearly the third symptom of capitalism-in-decay, British Fascism, was important as a reflection of what was happening in Italy and Germany rather than as a factor in British politics. The movement never had anything like the influence, for example, of the extreme right-wing French party Action Française, which had been founded in 1899, was especially important in the thirties, and was a prominent influence on the Vichy government of France during the German occupation.

Sir Oswald Mosley founded the British Union of Fascists in 1932 (there had been earlier groups), and by 1934 it had 400 branches in various parts of the country. It was, briefly, supported by the *Daily Mail* whose owner, the then Lord Rothermere, wrote in its pages in 1934:

> At this next vital election Britain's survival as a Great Power will depend on the existence of a well-organized Party of the Right, ready to take over responsibility for national affairs with the same directness of purpose and energy of method as Mussolini and Hitler have displayed.

The Union of Fascists' most famous moment came in June 1934, when it staged a public meeting at Olympia in London at which hecklers were openly beaten up. Mosley also organized provocative, uniformed marches through the London East End where there was a strong Jewish and Communist element—the so-called battles of Cable Street and Mile End Road, which are described in Wesker's play *Chicken Soup with Barley*, took place in 1936.

In *The Road to Wigan Pier* Orwell discussed the possibility that a depressed middle class, lost to socialism by silly Marxist tactics of bourgeois-baiting, might go over to some form of British Fascism. But eyes generally were on the doings of Hitler and Mussolini rather than on those of Mosley—just as they were on the doings of Stalin and Molotov rather than on those of Palme Dutt or Harry Pollitt in the British Communist Party.

Hitler took Germany out of the League of Nations in 1933 (Japan, whose forces had marched into Manchuria two years before, also left in that year). In 1935 he passed the Nuremberg Laws (which denied Jews German citizenship, and forbade them to marry 'Aryan' women), and admitted a policy of re-armament. In the same year Mussolini invaded Abyssinia. Also in the same year the British Home Office began to distribute leaflets on air-raid precautions, and a White Paper on Defence said of Germany: 'The spirit in which the population and especially the youth of the country are being organized lends colour to . . . the general feeling of insecurity'. In 1936 Hitler marched into the demilitarized zone of the Rhineland, and both he and Mussolini were finding the Spanish Civil War to be a useful training ground for technicians and military personnel. By March of that year the *New Statesman* had noted:

> We cannot too explicitly state our view that without a profound modification of the Nazi régime—and there are moderate as well as revolutionary forces in the Nazi régime—there can be no peace in Europe, but only a terrified waiting for war.

But the moderate forces were to have no say in the events to follow. A triangular pact against international communism was signed by Germany, Italy and Japan in 1937. In 1938 Jewish

38

property in Germany was confiscated and Austria was annexed—the Anschluss. One third of the population of Czechoslovakia and one of the biggest armament production centres in Europe were taken over by Hitler as a result of the agreement we know as 'Munich' (with 'means-test', this is one of the dirtiest words to emerge from the decade). Slit-trenches were dug in London parks; gas-masks were distributed. In 1939—when Orwell published his novel *Coming Up For Air*—Hitler marched into Prague, then into Poland, and an inter-war period of twenty-one years was over.

By the end of 1939 Orwell, in his middle thirties, had published seven books: four of them were novels, and three were mixtures of sociology, political analysis and autobiography. He had also published a handful of essays (including 'Shooting an Elephant', 'Dickens' and 'Boys' Weeklies'). He was known rather than famous; he had never made very much money from what he had written; he had only once reached a mass readership.

This first half of his writing career developed in a decade which was very fertile for English literature. As already suggested, the work that springs first to mind in connection with Orwell is that of the writers—all more or less his contemporaries—associated with the *New Writing* anthology: Auden, Isherwood, Spender, Day Lewis, MacNeice, Edward Upward. But this is also the decade which saw the appearance of new work by Eliot, Huxley, Greene, Waugh, Yeats, O'Casey, Virginia Woolf —and by Hemingway, Faulkner and Scott Fitzgerald. Or, to be less parochial, by Koestler, Malraux and Ignazio Silone, by Thomas Mann and André Gide. There is one book which as time passes seems increasingly to occupy a central place in modern European literature—Kafka's *The Trial*, which was written in 1925 and translated into English in 1937. Orwell never mentions the book, the symbolism of which was probably alien to him; but its theme—the destruction of an individual by the forces of some mysterious organization—was very much his own.

THE ADULT WORLD (II—1939–50)

When the Second World War started Orwell had just over ten

years left to live—years in which he produced the two pieces of fiction which made him famous, and the great majority of his essays.

Six of these remaining years were spent in a country fighting a war which in many ways came as a relief and as a clearing-up of issues after the confusion and shabby retreats of the previous years. It was a war in which Orwell believed that England could renew herself, and would have to do so by letting ordinary people get their hands on political power, if she was to survive. Domestically the war brought unity and direction. It brought shortage and austerity. It brought, of course, material damage and loss of life—although on nothing like the scale suffered by either Russia or Germany. No one in England experienced the equivalent of the Battle of Stalingrad or the fire-raid on Hamburg. The war also brought about the last stages of the welfare state when a Labour Government, for the first time with an over-all majority, put into operation the suggestions contained in William Beveridge's *Report on Social Insurance and Allied Services*, published in 1942.

In August 1945 at the opening of the new Parliament (it was the month in which the first atomic bomb was dropped) the Reply to the King's Speech suggested that the occasion might be regarded as D-day in the Battle for a New Britain. But the evolution of a full social democracy seemed to carry with it none of the excitement and glamour that Orwell had noted in northern Spain when he had lived alongside the Catalonian revolutionaries in the first months of 1937. There were growing financial problems caused by the immense cost of the war, food and fuel crises, shortages of this and that, a general shabbiness in everything. These things (and, apparently, conditions in the B.B.C. canteen during the war) were to contribute to the dreary atmosphere of *Nineteen Eighty-Four*.

By 1945 German and Italian Fascism had been defeated. By 1947 one of the major features of British imperialism—the one with which Orwell himself had been associated—had gone. India was independent and partitioned; Burma was independent and out of the Commonwealth. The defeat of the one and disappearance of the other authoritarianism made all the clearer the growth of a third. Behind what was now christened the Iron Curtain, stretching across eastern Europe, a victorious Stalinism began building up a chain of satellite states. Within Russia itself there was a re-imposition of a Party-discipline which had been relaxed during the war, a new stress on the need for orthodoxy and the closer control of ideology. One aspect of this —of special concern to Orwell himself, as a writer—was the increased control of literature, expressed in such a statement as the following Decree of the Communist Party Central Committee in August, 1946:

> The Soviet system cannot tolerate the education of youth in a spirit of indifference to Soviet politics, to ideology, with a couldn't-care-less attitude. The strength of Soviet literature, the most advanced literature in the world, consists in the fact that it is a literature in which there are not and cannot be interests other than the interests of the people, the interests of the state. The task of Soviet literature is to help the state to educate youth correctly, to answer its requirements, to bring up the new generation to be strong, believing in its cause, not fearing obstacles, ready to overcome all obstacles.

Add to this the physical sadism and it does not seem very far from what O'Brien tells Winston Smith in the Ministry of Love, in *Nineteen Eighty-Four*.

Much of Europe had been spiritually and physically obliterated. One historian estimates that twenty-five million soldiers and twenty-four million civilians were killed during the war. Many were left starving or 'displaced' after it. Frightful documents and photographs were emerging from the archives at Auschwitz and Buchenwald as they were needed at the Nuremberg war trials; a new weapon that altered the whole scale of war had been used in Asia; the United Nations seemed to be going the same way as the League of Nations which it had replaced. Another aggressive totalitarianism was apparently preparing itself in Europe (the Berlin Blockade began in 1948). Events seemed to continue to run in the pattern of the age of violence—and by now Orwell himself was seriously ill.

In June 1950, four months after he had died, Orwell was commemorated in a periodical called *World Review*. Introducing the issue, Bertrand Russell wrote this:

Our age calls for a greater energy of belief than was needed in the eighteenth and nineteenth centuries. Imagine Goethe, Shelley and Wells confined for years to Buchenwald; how would they emerge? Obviously not as they went in. Goethe would no longer be 'the Olympian', nor Shelley the 'ineffectual angel', and Wells would have lost his belief in the omnipotence of reason. . . . The men of our day who resemble Goethe, Shelley or Wells in temperament and congenital capacity have mostly gone through, either personally or through imaginative sympathy, experiences more or less resembling imprisonment in Buchenwald. Orwell was one of these men. He preserved an impeccable love of truth, and allowed himself to learn even the most painful lessons. But he lost hope. This prevented him from being a prophet for our time. Perhaps it is impossible, in the world as it is, to combine hope with truth; if so, all prophets must be false prophets. For my part, I lived too long in a happier world to be able to accept so glowing★ a doctrine. I find in men like Orwell the half, but only the half, of what the world needs; the other half is still to seek.

★ 'glowing' is a misprint for 'gloomy'.

3

Basic Attitudes

P. G. Wodehouse said in a television interview that Orwell looked the sort of fellow who would never be happy, and in a world of social disintegration accompanied by the helplessness of all decent people Orwell did find very little to be happy about. He wrote to a fellow Old Etonian: 'I have had a bloody life a good deal of the time, but in some ways an interesting one.'

Only occasionally (for example, when he read the works of George Gissing with their pictures of the horrors of English life in the eighteen-eighties and -nineties, or when he remembered cosy working-class interiors as he had seen them in his youth) would he admit that his age was not an altogether bad one to live in. More characteristic is a remark such as the one in his essay on Arthur Koestler (1944) where, after declaring that 'Nothing is in sight except a welter of lies, hatred, cruelty and ignorance, and beyond our present troubles loom vaster ones', he concluded that some degree of suffering was ineradicable from human life.

In 1937, after his experience with the unemployed miners in the north of England, he described a mess so serious that even the dullest-witted could not ignore it:

> We are living in a world in which nobody is free, in which hardly anybody is secure, in which it is almost impossible to be honest and to remain alive. . . . And this is merely a preliminary stage, in a country still rich with the loot of a hundred years. Presently there may be coming God knows what horrors—horrors of which, in this sheltered island, we have not even a traditional knowledge.
>
> RWP 170; P 149

In a long essay called 'Inside the Whale' (1940) he compared 20th-century Europe with the America of Walt Whitman:

> To say 'I accept' in an age like our own is to say that you accept concentration camps, rubber truncheons, Hitler, Stalin, bombs, aeroplanes, tinned food, machine guns, putsches, purges, slogans, Bedaux belts, gas masks, submarines, spies, provocateurs, press censorship, secret prisons, aspirins, Hollywood films, and political murders. Not *only* those things, of course, but those things among others. . . . unquestionably our own age, at any rate in Western Europe, is less healthy and less hopeful than the age in which Whitman was writing. Unlike Whitman, we live in a *shrinking* world. The 'democratic vistas' have ended in barbed wire. There is less feeling of creation and growth, less and less emphasis on the cradle, endlessly rocking, more and more emphasis on the teapot, endlessly stewing. To accept civilization *as it is* practically means accepting decay.   EYE 102; COL E 126

In 1947 he told T. R. Fyvel, his successor as literary editor of *Tribune*, that a war was coming in the next ten or twenty years in which England would disappear: 'The only hope is to have a home with a few animals in some place not worth a bomb.'

The 20th century seemed to have succumbed to the powers of medieval barbarism, and those who tried to understand it in the terms of post-Renaissance rationalism and science had no hope of doing so. In 'Wells, Hitler and the World State' (1941) there is this comment on the author whose works he had read as a schoolboy:

> He was, and still is, quite incapable of understanding that nationalism, religious bigotry and feudal loyalty are far more powerful forces than what he himself would describe as sanity. Creatures out of the Dark Ages have come marching into the present, and if they are ghosts they are at any rate ghosts which need a strong magic to lay them. . . . Wells is too sane to understand the modern world.   CE 98; COL E 165

The science which in Wells' own prime at the turn of the century could justifiably be regarded as the symbol of sanity was now allied to the Dark Age creatures. The aeroplane, looked forward to as an instrument of civilization, was used only for bombing;

modern Germany, much more scientific than England, was also much more barbarous.

Orwell sometimes contrasted his experience of his own period and locality with his literary experience of 19th-century America, where men felt themselves free and equal, where (except for the Negroes) there was no permanently submerged class, and where you could earn a decent living without boot-licking. The heroes of such American literature seemed more remote than Stone Age cannibals:

> The reason is simply that they are free human beings. . . . life has a buoyant, carefree quality that you can feel as you read, like a physical sensation in your belly. EYE 101; COL E 125

On the other hand, the modern European world was character-ized by planning—and the planners destroyed individual freedom; by revolution—and revolutionary leaders in their corruption seemed to replace one tyranny by a worse; by the worship of power—and power destroyed righteousness.

Orwell's own experience in Burma as a wielder of power, preventing men from feeling free and equal ('. . . in the police you see the dirty work of Empire at close quarters'), left him, when he resigned, in a condition such as this:

> I was conscious of an immense weight of guilt that I had got to expiate. . . . I had reduced everything to the simple theory that the oppressed are always right and the oppressors are always wrong: a mistaken theory, but the natural result of being one of the op-pressors yourself. I felt that I had got to escape not merely from imperialism but from every form of man's dominion over man. I wanted to submerge myself, to get right down among the oppressed, to be one of them and on their side against their tyrants. . . . Once I had been among them and accepted by them [Orwell is now talking of social outcasts], I should have touched bottom, and—this is what I felt: I was aware even then that it was irrational—part of my guilt would drop from me. RWP 149; P 129

One of the most revealing statements he ever made comes from a description of his police work in Burma: 'I never went into a jail without feeling (most visitors to jails feel the same) that my place

45

was really on the other side of the bars'—the knowing and quite unfounded generalization in the parenthesis is also typical. This is the ex-policeman who was later to write in connection with his involvement in street-fighting in Barcelona: '. . . when I see an actual flesh-and-blood worker in conflict with his natural enemy, the policeman, I do not have to ask myself which side I am on.'

Looking back on his childhood in the lower upper middle class (part of the wreckage left behind when Victorian prosperity receded), Orwell suggested that it had been lived on two levels simultaneously. You knew about tipping servants, but had hardly any to tip; you knew how to wear decent clothes and order a good meal, but could never afford to do either. It was like being a Poor White in a street full of Negroes. Looking back on his schooldays, he saw them as on the one hand making him cling more tenaciously to his gentility while on the other making him resent the boys who were richer than he was. Such a sense of dislocation—this is roughly the period of the First World War—with the added guilt brought about by his work in Burma seems to have made him one of those outsiders or 'alienated men' who have figured so largely in modern European literature and criticism.

He felt a need to associate himself, both really and imaginatively, with the outcasts and victims: the ugly, smelly, poor boy at the snobbish prep. school; the browbeaten Burmese; the *plongeurs* and tramps of Paris and London; the unemployed miners of Lancashire and Yorkshire; the persecuted dissident Marxists of Barcelona; the protagonists of his novels like Dorothy Hare, Flory, Comstock, Bowling and Winston Smith; the deprived writer in the authoritarian 'Leviathan' state. Even as a believer in Socialism he had to be an anti-Socialist.

In the world of 20th-century barbarism—manifested in capitalist industrialization, in the worship of power and admiration for violence, in Communist or Fascist totalitarianism, in the destruction of the writer's freedom—the only thing to do was to rebel. In this way could be carried on what Orwell quoted E. M. Forster as calling 'the human tradition', for which his own phrase was 'common decency'. Although the rebellion always failed, it always continued. The vision of men living in brotherhood—whether it was called the Kingdom of Heaven or the Classless Society—never materialized, but belief in it never seemed to die out.

Sometimes, however, liberty, equality and fraternity looked like becoming as old-fashioned as the French Revolution of which they had been a part. The present world was not one in which the individual could expand, but one in which he was usually enslaved or liquidated. Orwell's work can be seen as beginning in 1931 with a description of a man being hanged by the authorities: 'He and we were a party of men walking together, seeing, hearing, feeling, understanding the same world; and in two minutes, with a sudden snap, one of us would be gone—one mind less, one world less.' It can be seen as ending in 1949 with the more sophisticated destruction of Winston Smith: 'But it was all right, everything was all right, the struggle was finished. He had won the victory over himself. He loved Big Brother.' In 1935 Orwell wrote a poem of which these are the opening and closing stanzas:

> A happy vicar I might have been
> Two hundred years ago,
> To preach upon eternal doom
> And watch my walnuts grow;
>
> But born, alas, in an evil time,
> I missed that pleasant haven,
> For the hair has grown on my upper lip
> And the clergy are all clean-shaven.
>
> .   .   .   .   .
>
> I dreamed I dwelt in marble halls,
> And woke to find it true;
> I wasn't born for an age like this;
> Was Smith? Was Jones? Were you?   EYE 12; COL E 423

GOD AND MAN

This frustrated vicar once or twice described his time's major problem as that of the decay of the belief in personal immortality.

47

Yet no one would consider Orwell to be a religious writer and (apart from that in his early novel, *A Clergyman's Daughter*) he gave this 'major problem' very little continuous discussion. He argued that it could not be tackled until material privation and brute labour had been abolished. In his essay on Koestler, he quotes that writer's description of himself as a short-term pessimist believing that the present horrors would eventually clear, and comments that such an outlook results from the difficulty (in an irreligious person) of accepting earthly life as something inherently miserable, and the realization that to make life liveable is a much bigger problem than it seemed:

> It is quite possible that man's major problems will *never* be solved. But it is also unthinkable! . . . The only easy way out is that of the religious believer, who regards this life merely as a preparation for the next. But few thinking people now believe in life after death, and the number of those who do is probably diminishing. . . . The real problem is how to restore the religious attitude [to life] while accepting death as final. CE 161; COL E 231

By the religious attitude to life Orwell seems to mean an acceptance that happiness is not the object of human existence. He develops the idea of the finality of death in an article, written about the same time, published in *Tribune* on 3rd March 1944:

> There is little doubt that the modern cult of power-worship is bound up with the modern man's feeling that life here and now is the only life there is. If death ends everything, it becomes much harder to believe that you can be in the right even if you are defeated. Statesmen, nations, theories, causes are judged almost inevitably by the test of material success. Supposing that one can separate the two phenomena, I would say that the decay of the belief in personal immortality has been as important as the rise of machine civilization. . . . I do not want the belief in life after death to return, and in any case it is not likely to return. What I do point out is that its disappearance has left a big hole, and that we ought to take notice of that fact. . . . One cannot have any worthwhile picture of the future unless one realizes how much we have lost by the decay of Christianity.

The psychological effort of adapting himself to the idea that he perishes, necessary if man was to salvage civilization, meant the evolution of an ethical system independent of a belief in heaven and hell, as had been achieved by Marxism.

Two articles published just over a year later in *The Observer* for 10th June and 22nd July argued similarly and suggested that the material progress made possible by machinery had been achieved at a fearful cost. On the one hand, supernatural beliefs had brought exploitation by priests and oligarchs, and the hindrance of technical development; on the other, replacing worship of God by worship of Man had been disastrous. Any humanist had to decide whether what was needed was re-education and a change of heart, or the abolition of poverty. From his essay on Dickens it is clear that Orwell had sympathy with the first view, but in the end he usually decided that working-class materialism was right in placing the belly before the soul—in point of time if not in scale of values. Men were only as good as their technical development allowed them to be.

Human beings, he suggested in 'Reflections on Gandhi' (1949), had to avoid sainthood's inhuman demands:

> The essence of being human is that one does not seek perfection, that one *is* sometimes willing to commit sins for the sake of loyalty, that one does not push asceticism to the point where it makes friendly intercourse impossible. . . . it is not necessary here to argue whether the other-worldly or the humanist ideal is 'higher'. The point is that they are incompatible. One must choose between God and Man, and all 'radicals' and 'progressives', from the mildest Liberal to the most extreme Anarchist, have in effect chosen Man.
> SE 108

Having chosen the world of Man you must not be surprised if, when you throw away your weapons, some less scrupulous person picks them up; or if, when you turn the other cheek, you get a harder blow on it than you did on the first. In 'Looking Back on the Spanish War' (1943) Orwell noted that to survive you have to fight and dirty yourself: 'War is evil, and it is often the lesser evil. Those who take the sword perish by the sword, and those who don't take the sword perish by smelly diseases.'

In the introduction to *British Pamphleteers*, Orwell described capitalism as a progressive event only insofar as it could lead eventually to a Socialist society. Considering its actual achievements—'the destruction of one culture after another, the piling-up of millions of human beings in hideous ant-heaps of cities, and, above all, the enslavement of the coloured races'—it was difficult to regard it as superior to the feudalism it replaced.

Capitalism, a competitive system motivated by private profit and resulting in economic chaos, simply could not deliver the goods, as seemed to be proved in England by the course of the Second World War before the evacuation of Dunkirk. Such a system was doomed; the only question was whether it would be replaced by true democracy or by the rule of the power élites.

The capitalist industrialization inherited from the 19th century meant a society based on a kind of civil war. On one side was the enslaved poor, such as the Parisian dish-washer; on the other was the educated rich man superstitiously fearful of what he called the mob:

> The educated man pictures a horde of submen, wanting only a day's liberty to loot his house, burn his books, and set him to work minding a machine or sweeping out a lavatory. 'Anything,' he thinks, 'any injustice, sooner than let that mob loose.' He does not see that since there is no difference between the mass of rich and poor, there is no question of setting the mob loose. The mob is in fact loose now, and—in the shape of rich men—is using its power to set up enormous treadmills of boredom, such as 'smart' hotels.

DOPL 120; P 108

This society made possible—or inevitable—such people as the Brookers, who kept the gruesome lodging house described at the beginning of *The Road to Wigan Pier*, such urban landscapes as those of Lancashire and Yorkshire: 'labyrinthine slums and dark back kitchens with sickly, ageing people creeping round and round them like blackbeetles.'

The same industrialization was producing a mechanized society in more than a literal sense—and, here, in his attitude that the tendency of the machine is to make a fully human life impossible,

Orwell joins a tradition extending from Blake to D. H. Lawrence. (The brain-in-a-bottle reference in the following extract probably refers to Huxley's *Brave New World*.) Everywhere is the machine cutting you off from the work which satisfies the human need for effort and creation:

> Therefore the logical end of mechanical progress is to reduce the human being to something resembling a brain in a bottle. That is the goal towards which we are already moving, though, of course, we have no intention of getting there. . . . The implied objective of 'progress' is—not *exactly*, perhaps, the brain in the bottle, but at any rate some frightful subhuman depth of softness and helplessness.
>
> RWP 200; P 176

In an essay called 'Pleasure Spots', published in *Tribune*, 11th January 1946, continuing the argument, Orwell describes the future mechanical paradise as something already to be partially glimpsed on a modern pleasure cruise or in a Lyons Corner House: the impossibility of being alone, of doing anything for oneself, of seeing anything natural, of being silent:

> It is difficult not to feel that the unconscious aim in the most typical modern pleasure resorts is a return to the womb . . . [if we recognized this] the instinctive horror which all sensitive people feel at the progressive mechanization of life would be seen not to be a mere sentimental archaism, but to be fully justified. For man only stays human by preserving large patches of simplicity in his life, while the tendency of many modern inventions—in particular the film, the radio and the aeroplane—is to weaken his consciousness, dull his curiosity, and, in general, drive him nearer to the animals.

But hatred of the machine, however correct, could not involve the question of its acceptance or rejection: it was here to stay. It was clear that equality was possible only in a society on a high technical level—even if achieving this meant the destruction of taste and the involvement of everyone in a frighteningly automatic 'progress'. And yet, the sensitive man's unrealistic attitude to the machine had much to be said for it:

> The machine has got to be accepted, but it is probably better to accept it rather as one accepts a drug—that is, grudgingly and

suspiciously. Like a drug, the machine is useful, dangerous, and habit-forming. The oftener one surrenders to it the tighter its grip becomes. You have only to look about you at this moment to realize with what sinister speed the machine is getting us into its power.   RWP 202; P 178

In its later stages, according to Lenin, capitalism's struggle for external markets produced that system of colonial oppression known as imperialism. Orwell admitted that the agents of Britain's monstrous intrusion into India and Burma had got things done. In his essay on Kipling (1942), he wrote of the 19th-century sahibs that, even if all they did was evil, they had changed the face of the earth, whereas they would have achieved nothing on the basis of a liberal humanism like E. M. Forster's.

But, in an admittedly benevolent despotism which had theft as its final object, power did terrible things to the individuals involved, oppressors as well as oppressed. The police-official of 'Shooting an Elephant' (1936), trying to decide whether or not to shoot the beast in front of a crowd of excited Burmese, is no more in control of the situation than they are, as he realizes the futility of white dominion in the East:

> I perceived in this moment that when the white man turns tyrant it is his own freedom that he destroys. He becomes a sort of hollow, posing dummy, the conventionalized figure of a sahib. . . . He wears a mask, and his face grows to fit it.   SE 6; COL E 19

The masked existence forced on the sahibs made their lives stifled and stultified. Few of them seemed to work as hard or as intelligently as a provincial postmaster. In the constant playing of their role, every word and thought had to undergo censorship in an atmosphere difficult to conceive from England:

> . . . even friendship can hardly exist when every white man is a cog in the wheels of despotism. Free speech is unthinkable. All other kinds of freedom are permitted. You are free to be a drunkard, an idler, a coward, a backbiter, a fornicator; but you are not free to think for yourself. Your opinion on every subject of any conceivable importance is dictated for you by the pukka sahibs' code.
>
> BD 69; P 66

The more obviously destroyed were the natives themselves—bullied, exploited, reduced to the level of things. In his essay 'Marrakech' (1939), Orwell noted as one of the facts on which empires are founded how difficult it had been, while walking through the Moroccan town, to understand that he was among human beings. People with brown skins were next to invisible; and there are so many of them. 'Are they really the same flesh as yourself? Do they even have names? Or are they merely a kind of undifferentiated brown stuff, about as individual as bees or coral insects?'

By its possession of a coolie empire at the same time as it made pious and affluent democratic noises, Britain was placed in an equivocal position. This was even truer of the British left wing. Such parties were at bottom a sham, hypocritically accepting a standard of living based on the exploitation of undifferentiated brown stuff. Orwell makes the point when he is discussing Kipling: radical parties pretend to have internationalist aims, and yet struggle for a standard of life incompatible with them:

> We all live by robbing Asiatic coolies, and those of us who are 'enlightened' all maintain that those coolies ought to be set free; but our standard of living, and hence our 'enlightenment', demands that the robbery shall continue.   CE 115

After the First World War it was obvious that British imperialism was dying. It had been bad, but as the years passed it also became obvious that it had been better than the 'younger empires' of the rising totalitarian states that looked as if they were going to replace it.

TOTALITARIANISM, POWER AND VIOLENCE

'Totalitarianism' is a word out of favour with political theorists because it includes such different forms as Stalinist Communism and Hitlerite Fascism, which they must be very careful to separate. But Orwell himself frequently used it as a blanket term, as he used the word 'Fascist'—which he realized had become an almost entirely meaningless hate-word that different people at different times had applied to farmers, foxhunters,

53

shop-keepers, back-bench Conservatives, homosexuals, Kipling, Gandhi, Chiang Kai-shek, J. B. Priestley, Youth Hostels, astrology, women and dogs. In a *Tribune* article discussing these applications of the term Orwell concluded that, roughly speaking, it meant 'something cruel, unscrupulous, arrogant, obscurantist, anti-liberal and anti-working class . . . almost any English person would accept "bully" as a synonym for "Fascist"'.

In *The Road to Wigan Pier* he described Fascism as aiming at a world without private profit-making, but with power in the hands of an élite caste of rulers: a world of rabbits ruled by stoats. Thus Nazi Germany was a form of capitalism borrowing enough Socialism to make it an efficient war-machine, based on an elaborate caste system: the inner élite of the Party Members; the outer élite of the whole German people; the expendable slaves who were the conquered Europeans; and the semi-apes— the Slavs and Jews who were to be exterminated.

Such a totalitarian, authoritarian or 'Fascist' state is one in which private relationships and principles are minimized or destroyed. All responsibilities are public ones conditioned by duty to the State. In Huxley's *Brave New World* the motto of the World State is 'Community, Identity, Stability'; in a novel called *We* by the Russian émigré writer Zamyatin (this book was probably one of the sources of Huxley's novel; Orwell himself reviewed it) it is said that in this kind of society nobody is ever 'one' but always 'one of'. Orwell used the word 'nationalism' in this sense to describe the insane modern habit of assuming that human beings were classifiable like insects; and that everything could be seen in terms of large power units with which the self must be identified, and the prestige of which must be constantly upheld by aggressive acts against other power units. It was in this aggressiveness that 'nationalism' differed from the more purely defensive attitude of 'patriotism'. 'One prod to the nerve of nationalism,' he wrote in his essay on the subject, 'and the intellectual decencies can vanish.'

Instead of merely forbidding certain activities (which always allowed the individual to practise some eccentricity), the nationalist or bee-hive society called upon perversions of 'love'

54

or 'reason' as a means of exerting continuous pressure towards solidarity. The aspect of this pressure that came most to alarm Orwell was that the novelty of totalitarianism lay in the muta-bility as well as the unchallengeability of its dogmas. These had to be accepted on pain of damnation, but were always liable to be altered at a moment's notice. In 'The Prevention of Literature' (1946) he wrote that the organized lying practised by totalitarian states was not merely a temporary expedient:

> It is something integral to totalitarianism, something that would still continue even if concentration camps and secret police forces had ceased to be necessary. . . . From the totalitarian point of view history is something to be created rather than learned. . . . Total-itarianism demands, in fact, the continuous alteration of the past, and in the long run probably demands a disbelief in the very existence of objective truth. SE 120; COL E 314

Whatever this kind of system is called (in *Nineteen Eighty-Four* it is known as 'oligarchical collectivism'), it was still the rule of the stoats. In 'W. B. Yeats' (1943) Orwell writes of a poet whom he saw as 'a great hater of democracy, of the modern world, science, machinery, the concept of progress':

> The merely political Fascist claims always to be fighting for justice: Yeats, the poet, sees at a glance that Fascism means injustice, and acclaims it for that very reason. But at the same time he fails to see that the new authoritarian civilization, if it arrives, will not be aristocratic, or what he means by aristocratic. It will not be ruled by noblemen with Van Dyck faces, but by anonymous millionaires, shiny-bottomed bureaucrats and murdering gangsters.

CE 133; COL E 183

It was a nightmare world, but could not be written off as merely that, for in 1925 the actual world of the nineteen-forties would have seemed nightmarish. Indeed this particular nightmare of the régime of the millionaire-bureaucrat-gangster was firmly rooted in the amoral development of the 20th century. In 'Rudyard Kipling' (1942) Orwell says:

> No-one, in our time, believes in any sanction greater than military power: no-one believes that it is possible to overcome force except

55

by greater force. There is no 'law', there is only power. I am not saying that that is a true belief, merely that it is the belief which all modern men do actually hold. Those who pretend otherwise are either intellectual cowards, or power-worshippers under a thin disguise, or have simply not caught up with the age they are living in.

CE 114

Although mass-literature like the boys' weeklies was mostly 'sodden in the worst illusions of 1910', there were manifestations of a later bully-worship and cult of violence. The American ideal of the he-man ('the gorilla who puts everything right by socking everybody else on the jaw') had emerged as a central figure. Similarly an Americanized shocker like *No Orchids for Miss Blandish*, particularly when compared with an old-fashioned, gentlemanly affair like *Raffles*, presented a day-dream appropriate to a totalitarian age. In 'Raffles and Miss Blandish' (1944), Orwell analyses a thriller where he finds no hint of affection, good nature or even ordinary politeness. The pursuit of power—the fashionable doctrine of 'realism'—is the only motive at work:

> Until recently the characteristic adventure stories of the English-speaking peoples have been stories in which the hero fights *against odds*. This is true all the way from Robin Hood to Pop-eye the Sailor. Perhaps the basic myth of the Western world is Jack the Giant-killer, but to be brought up to date this should be renamed Jack the Dwarf-killer, and there already exists a considerable literature which teaches, either overtly or implicitly, that one should side with the big man against the little man. . . . In his imagined world of gangsters Chase is presenting, as it were, a distilled version of the modern political scene, in which such things as mass bombing of civilians, the use of hostages, torture to obtain confessions, secret prisons, execution without trial, floggings with rubber truncheons, drownings in cesspools, systematic falsification of records and statistics, treachery, bribery and quislingism are normal and morally neutral, even admirable when they are done in a large and bold way.
> CE 176; COL E 245

DECENCY AND SOCIALISM

'His whole "message",' Orwell wrote of Dickens, 'is one that at first glance looks like an enormous platitude: If men would behave decently the world would be decent'—which he later concludes 'is not necessarily so shallow as it sounds'. But in the modern world 'realism' (or callous expediency and the excitements of violence) had replaced decency. Cricket, with its concepts of good form and playing the game, had declined, along with the tradition of not hitting a man when he is down: 'It is not a 20th-century game,' he noted in 'Raffles and Miss Blandish', 'nearly all modern-minded people dislike it.' The only way out of the moral pig-sty was to understand that realism did not pay, that there were prudential reasons for decency, and that on the whole men could not behave decently until they were part of a decent system. The only way of achieving a decent system was through Socialism:

> Nothing else can save us from the misery of the present [1936] or the nightmare of the future. To oppose Socialism *now*, when twenty million Englishmen are underfed and Fascism has conquered half Europe, is suicidal. It is like starting a civil war when the Goths are crossing the frontier. RWP 218; P 193

In England, between the General Strike of 1926 and the start of the Second World War, Socialism was the chance of the common people to escape from their traditional role of being acted upon by others, the passive victims of 'their' realism. In Europe of the same period, Socialism seemed to be the best chance of stopping Hitler, Mussolini and Franco.

There was nothing intellectually doctrinaire about Orwell's politics. He related how it seemed to him on his return from Burma that economic injustice would stop as soon as we genuinely wanted it to, 'and if we genuinely want it to stop the method adopted hardly matters'. He was willing to regard anyone 'who knows the meaning of poverty, everyone who has a genuine hatred of tyranny and war' as potentially on the Socialist side. With its 'nonsense' stripped off, Socialism meant that justice and liberty for which we now had to fight:

> To the ordinary working man . . . Socialism does not mean much more than better wages and shorter hours and nobody bossing you about. To the more revolutionary type . . . the word is a sort of

57

rallying-cry against the forces of oppression, a vague threat of future violence. But, so far as my experience goes, no genuine working man grasps the deeper implications of Socialism. Often, in my opinion, he is a truer Socialist than the orthodox Marxist, because he does remember, what the other so often forgets, that Socialism means justice and common decency.　　　　　RWP 176; P 154

I am well aware that it is now the fashion to deny that Socialism has anything to do with equality. In every country in the world a huge tribe of party-hacks and sleek little professors are busy 'proving' that Socialism means no more than a planned state-capitalism with the grab-motive left intact. But fortunately there also exists a vision of Socialism quite different from this. The thing that attracts ordinary men to Socialism and makes them willing to risk their skins for it, the 'mystique' of Socialism, is the idea of equality; to the vast majority of people Socialism means a classless society, or it means nothing at all.　　　　　HC 111; P 102

Such emotional Socialism meant a movement basing itself upon the Marseillaise rather than on Marxism, a movement that was a league of the oppressed against oppressors rather than of burbling dialectical materialists whose signature tune was 'Fee fi fo fum, I smell the blood of a right-wing deviationist'. Thus Orwell does not often talk about the details of a Socialist society. The following is a fairly isolated example:

Socialism is usually defined as 'common ownership of the means of production'. Crudely: the State, representing the whole nation, owns everything, and everyone is a State employee. This does *not* mean that people are stripped of private possessions such as clothes and furniture, but it *does* mean that all productive goods, such as land, mines, ships and machinery, are the property of the State. The State is the sole large-scale producer. It is not certain that Socialism is in all ways superior to capitalism, but it is certain that, unlike capitalism, it can solve the problems of production and consumption. . . . One must also add the following: approximate equality of incomes . . . political democracy, and abolition of all hereditary privilege, especially in education. These are simply the necessary safeguards against the reappearance of a class system.　　LU 48

The centre of Orwell's concern with Socialism was that during the thirties it seemed everywhere to be in retreat. This was partly because of its association with merely material progress ('making the world safe for little fat men'); partly because the mistaken tactic of bourgeois-baiting had antagonized the middle classes whose support was essential and who otherwise might go over to Fascism; partly because of bad Socialist propaganda and silly Socialists:

> Justice and liberty! *Those* are the words that have got to ring like a bugle across the world. For a long time past, certainly for the last ten years, the devil has had all the best tunes. We have reached a stage when the very word 'Socialism' calls up, on the one hand, a picture of aeroplanes, tractors, and huge glittering factories of glass and concrete; on the other, a picture of vegetarians with wilting beards, of Bolshevik commissars (half gangster, half gramophone), of earnest ladies in sandals, shock-headed Marxists chewing poly-syllables, escaped Quakers, birth-control fanatics, and Labour Party backstairs-crawlers. Socialism, at least in this island, does not smell any longer of revolution and the overthrow of tyrants; it smells of crankishness, machine-worship, and the stupid cult of Russia. Unless you can remove that smell, and very rapidly, Fascism may win. RWP 214; P 190

After twenty years of stagnation and unemployment in England, the entire English Socialist movement had not yet produced a version of the creed emotionally attractive to the mass of the people. Orwell believed it a frightful comment on the Labour Party that in a moment of disaster like 1940 the people still looked to a Conservative for leadership. 'You have got to make it clear,' he wrote in *The Road to Wigan Pier*, which was written for a left-wing reading public, 'that there is room in the Socialist movement for human beings or the game is up.' And in bleaker moments it looked as if the game was up. In 'Inside the Whale' (1940), he noted the break-up of *laissez-faire* capitalism and of liberal-Christian culture, and prophesied a move into an age of totalitarian dictatorship 'in which freedom of thought will be at first a deadly sin and later on a meaningless abstraction'. It had been imagined that Socialism could preserve and enlarge the atmosphere of liberalism; 'it is now beginning to be realized how false this idea was'.

Orwell believed the salient features of the English people were artistic insensibility, suspicion of foreigners, sentimentality over animals, hypocrisy, exaggerated class-consciousness, obsession with sport, and respect for legality and gentleness. There may be a certain amount of petty persecution, but the real totalitarian atmosphere was hardly imaginable. The English were an old-fashioned people, out of step with modern European 'realism' to which they opposed

> ... not another theory of their own, but a moral quality which must be vaguely described as decency. .... The outstanding and—by contemporary standards—highly original quality of the English is their habit of *not killing one another*. Putting aside the 'model' small states, which are in an exceptional position, England is the only European country where internal politics are conducted in a more or less humane and decent manner. It is—and this was true long before the rise of Fascism—the only country where armed men do not prowl the streets and no one is frightened of the secret police.　　　　　　　　　　　　　　　　　　　　EP 40

The truly native culture was unofficial and private, based on an almost 19th-century belief in the freedom of the individual. Unlike the more cosmopolitan intelligentsia, the common people had not caught up with power politics. They still believed in justice, liberty and objective truth; they still lived in the spiritual world of Dickens with its human decency and sympathy for the under-dog. This old-fashionedness made England the last defence of democracy against continental totalitarianism:

> So long as democracy exists, even in its very imperfect English form, totalitarianism is in deadly danger. The whole English-speaking world is haunted by the idea of human equality, and though it would be simply a lie to say that either we or the Americans have ever acted up to our professions, still, the *idea* is there, and it is capable of one day becoming a reality. From the English-speaking culture, if it does not perish, a society of free and equal human beings will ultimately arise. .... With all its sloth, hypocrisy and injustice, the English-speaking civilization is the only large obstacle in Hitler's path. It is a living contradiction of all the 'infallible' dogmas of Fascism.　　　　　　　　　　　　　　LU 91

Sloth, hypocrisy and injustice; freedom, equality and privateness
—those were the contradictions in English life that had to be
resolved by making democracy Socialist. On the one side England
was 'a land of snobbery and privilege, ruled largely by the old
and silly'. On the other it possessed an emotional unity which
saw it through crisis after crisis:

> [England] resembles a family, a rather stuffy Victorian family, with
> not many black sheep in it but with all its cupboards bursting with
> skeletons. It has rich relations who have to be kow-towed to and
> poor relations who are horribly sat upon, and there is a deep
> conspiracy of silence about the source of the family income. It is a
> family in which the young are generally thwarted and most of the
> power is in the hands of irresponsible uncles and bed-ridden aunts.
> Still it is a family. It has its private language and its common mem-
> ories, and at the approach of an enemy it closes its ranks. A family
> with the wrong members in control—that, perhaps, is as near as one
> can come to describing England in a phrase.   LU 28

The English ruling classes—and whether they were wicked
or merely silly Orwell regarded as one of the most difficult as
well as one of the most important questions of his time—were
a generation of unteachables hanging round our necks like
corpses. They were not perhaps ultimately defeatist in the
struggle against Fascism, but there was always a possibility of
their pulling punches in the fight against a dictator they might
secretly regard as a defence against Russian Communism. Their
general attitude was that of the boys' weeklies (which Orwell
once suggested they used in order to inculcate similar attitudes
into working-class readers): it was perennially 1910 and the
British navy was in the Channel; nothing ever changed;
foreigners are funny.

Thus, the Second World War, really to Orwell a race between
the consolidation of Hitler's empire and the growth of
democratic consciousness, must become a revolutionary one.
England must be changed into a Socialist democracy where the
ordinary English people in the street had their hands on the
power. Patriots had to become revolutionists; revolutionists had
to become patriots—and this seemed to be possible at the time

of the withdrawal from Dunkirk:

> A Socialist movement which can swing the mass of the people behind it, drive the pro-Fascists out of positions of control, wipe out the grosser injustices and let the working class see that they have something to fight for, win over the middle classes instead of antagonizing them, produce a workable imperial policy instead of [a] mixture of humbug and Utopianism, bring patriotism and intelligence into partnership—for the first time, a movement of such a kind becomes possible. LU 73

Celebrating such an idea at the end of his wartime pamphlet *The Lion and the Unicorn*, he was moved to write with an uncharacteristic rhetoric:

> ... England has got to be true to herself. She is not being true to herself while the refugees who have sought our shores are penned up in concentration camps, and company directors work out subtle schemes to dodge their Excess Profits Tax. It is goodbye to the *Tatler* and the *Bystander*, and farewell to the lady in the Rolls-Royce car. The heirs of Nelson and of Cromwell are not in the House of Lords. They are in the fields and the streets, in the factories and the armed forces, in the four-ale bar and the suburban back garden; and at present they are still kept under by a generation of ghosts. Compared with the task of bringing the real England to the surface, even the winning of the war, necessary though it is, is secondary. By revolution we become more ourselves, not less. There is no question of stopping short, striking a compromise, salvaging 'democracy', standing still. Nothing ever stands still. We must add to our heritage or lose it, we must grow greater or grow less, we must go forward or backward. I believe in England, and I believe that we shall go forward. LU 96

INTELLECTUALS AND COMMUNISTS

Within the body of English people whom he trusted to go forward to Socialist Democracy was one group Orwell excepted —that of those left-wing intellectuals who tried to be anti-Fascist without being anti-totalitarian, and who since the time of Carlyle had cut themselves off from the national tradition by taking in bodies of continental ideas ultimately derived from the power-philosophy of Machiavelli.

62

An ordinary Englishman, Conservative, Socialist, Catholic, Communist, or what not, almost never grasps the full logical implications of the creed he professes: almost always he utters heresies without noticing it. Orthodoxies, whether of the Right or the Left, flourish chiefly among the literary intelligentsia, the people who ought in theory to be the guardians of freedom of thought. . . . English people in large numbers will not accept any creed whose dominant notes are hatred and illegality. The ruthless ideologies of the Continent—not merely Communism and Fascism, but Anarchism, Trotskyism, and even ultramontane Catholicism—are accepted in their pure form only by the intelligentsia, who constitute a sort of island of bigotry amid the general vagueness. EP 18

The mentality of these people could be studied in their periodicals: negative querulousness, lack of constructive suggestions, and emotional shallowness. Living in a world of ideas, having little contact with physical reality, undisciplined by any expectation of ever having to undertake responsibilities, this group acted as a kind of fifth column, as was suggested in 'Anti-Semitism in Britain' (1945): 'I do not think it an exaggeration to say that if the "intellectuals" had done their work a little more thoroughly, Britain would have surrendered in 1940.'

In a still broadly liberal society, where the right to free speech had to fight against economic pressure and public opinion but not, as yet, against the secret police, the intellectuals performed another kind of treason:

> . . . the conscious enemies of liberty are those to whom liberty ought to mean most. The big public do not care about the matter one way or the other. They are not in favour of persecuting the heretic, and they will not exert themselves to defend him. They are at once too sane and too stupid to acquire the totalitarian outlook. The direct, conscious attack on intellectual decency comes from the intellectuals themselves. SE 130; COL E 322

It was these same intellectuals who were destroying the fundamental nature of English Socialism, dehumanizing it, changing it into the Ingsoc of Oceania. Orwell in 'Second Thoughts on James Burnham' (1946) writes that the author of a book called *The Managerial Revolution* (which suggested that capitalism

63

would be replaced by the kind of super-state described in *Nineteen Eighty-Four*) is voicing the secret wish of the English intelligentsia: 'the wish to destroy the old, equalitarian version of Socialism and usher in a hierarchical society where the intellectual can at last get his hands on the whip.'

The allegiance and interest of such intellectuals (often those with the acutest vision), which ought to have been given to England, were more often given instead to the U.S.S.R. by a process which Orwell described as 'transferred nationalism'. Russia was the one great country where something described as a Socialist revolution had once happened, and where there had been a steady move away from the Socialist concepts of freedom, equality and universal brotherhood. This development had taken with it the Communist Party which, starting as a movement for the violent overthrow of capitalism, had degenerated into an instrument of Stalinist foreign policy, peddling a version of Socialism which made mental honesty impossible.

Orwell told Stephen Spender that he had been very hostile to the Party since 1935, and interestingly this is the year in which the Webbs published the most influentially pro-Soviet book of the period—*Soviet Communism—a New Civilization?* (the question mark was dropped in the second edition of 1937). At about the same time Harold Laski, a professor at the London School of Economics and at one time Chairman of the British Labour Party, lost his hostility to Communism and came to regard it as a centre of creativeness in Europe after the Depression and Hitler's rise to power. Orwell believed that such intellectuals were attracted to the movement partly by what he called the 'patriotism of the deracinated', but mainly by their ignorance—which he described in 'Inside the Whale':

> With all its injustices, England is still the land of habeas corpus, and the overwhelming majority of English people have no experience of violence or illegality. If you have grown up in that sort of atmosphere it is not at all easy to imagine what a despotic régime is like. Nearly all the dominant writers of the 'thirties belonged to the soft-boiled emancipated middle class and were too young to

have effective memories of the Great War. To people of that kind such things as purges, secret police, summary executions, imprisonment without trial, etc., etc., are too remote to be terrifying. They can swallow totalitarianism *because* they have no experience of anything except liberalism. . . . Hunger, hardship, solitude, exile, war, prison, persecution, manual labour—hardly even words. No wonder that the huge tribe known as 'the right left people' found it so easy to condone the purge-and-OGPU side of the Russian régime and the horrors of the first Five-Year Plan. They were so gloriously incapable of understanding what it all meant.

EYE 125; COL E 145

This is a very different picture from the one given at about the same time by the economist J. M. Keynes to the editor of the *New Statesman*. He described the same group of men as 'the nearest thing we now have to the typical nervous English gentleman who went to the Crusades, made the Reformation, fought the Great Rebellion, won us our civil and religious liberties and humanized the working classes last century'.

In one of his last essays, 'The Prevention of Literature' (1946), Orwell pulled together the two ends of the basic thread of his life—the struggle against tyranny—and wrote:

Fifteen years ago, when one defended the freedom of the intellect, one had to defend it against Conservatives, against Catholics, and to some extent—for they were not of great importance in England—against Fascists. Today one has to defend it against Communists and 'fellow-travellers'. . . . there can be no question about the poisonous effect of the Russian *mythos* on English intellectual life. Because of it known facts are suppressed and distorted to such an extent as to make it doubtful whether a true history of our times can ever be written.

SE 118; COL E 312

Perhaps all Orwell's books can be regarded as attempts to tell a true history of his times, but two—and many people regard them as the twin-summit of his achievement—come immediately to mind: *Homage to Catalonia* and *Animal Farm*. Seven years separated them, but taken together, as Orwell himself seems to have taken them, they crystallize most of the ideas presented in this chapter.

4

Two Histories of His Time

Spain became a republic in 1931—an event heralded by the British Labour Party as 'a ray of light and hope at a time when Fascism was trampling out liberty all over the world'. But this new republic saw no end to the turbulent disunity which had characterized the country ever since the Napoleonic conquest, and a good example of which can be found in the relationships that existed among its various left-wing parties.

In the 1936 elections to the Spanish parliament there came to power a Popular Front government which represented an alliance of the Socialist Party, two groups known as the Republican Left and the Republican Union, a group called the Esquerra (which wanted the northern province of Spain known as Catalonia to become a separate state), and the Communist Party. The Socialists were deeply divided over the question of how closely they were to cooperate with the Communists; the Communists themselves were splintered by the breaking away of anti-Stalinist 'Trotskyite' groups (which presented to the orthodox a much greater threat than did the right-wing Fascist parties, as they were traitors within the camp, defilers of the pure doctrine rather than merely its opponents). Outside parliament completely were the Anarchists who for decades had been at war with Spanish society in general, and who were traditional opponents of the Communists.

Thus, when the Spanish Civil War started it was not only a struggle between the anti-government forces of the Right and the pro-government forces of the Left; it was also a struggle within the Left itself. (An analogy might be seen in the position which developed in certain occupied countries during the Second World War—for example, in Poland or in Yugoslavia where there were two resistance groups fighting each other as well as the Germans.) It is with this internecine struggle among the parties ostensibly supporting the Spanish republic that Orwell was mainly concerned—especially so because his Spanish experience coincided with another, and very dramatic, example of such internecine warfare: the Moscow Purge Trials.

The Spanish Civil War began in the middle of July 1936, when General Franco organized a right-wing military rising against the government. In the consequent anti-Fascist rising to save the republic, the workers were formed into armed groups, based largely on their trade unions (these groups were known as militias). When the Franco revolt was temporarily crushed, these groups set about making a Socialist revolution. Meanwhile in August, at the first of the Moscow trials, Stalin began, by means of a gigantic distortion of the historical record, his systematic destruction of the 'Trotskyite' opposition within the Russian Communist Party. It is some indication of the ferocity of the whole purge that in it four hundred out of seven hundred generals were liquidated, as was seventy per cent of the Party Central Committee elected in 1934.

These two events at different ends of Europe, coming together as they did, formed a turning point in Orwell's life. They let him know where he stood. They provided him with experiences that most of his future work was to analyse through its concern with the related possibilities of left-wing dictatorship and the totalitarian destruction of historical truth. In one of his last essays ('Why I Write', 1946) he stated that every bit of serious work he had written since 1936 had been composed 'directly or indirectly, *against* totalitarianism and *for* democratic socialism, as I understand it'.

In Barcelona, after the preliminary fighting of July, an Anti-Fascist Militias Committee, made up of representatives from various groups on the left but dominated by the Anarchists, began the creation of a revolutionary society. Hotels, banks, stores and factories were closed or run by elected groups of former workers. Food distribution, farming, handicrafts and the cinemas were collectivized. All fifty-eight churches except the cathedral were burnt. To be seen wearing a tie was to risk arrest as a bourgeois. All this was done against a background of political assassination, plunder, destruction and growing hostility between the Anarchists and the Communists. By the end of July the latter were trying to disarm Anarchist militiamen in certain parts of the city; by the end of 1936 it was becoming obvious that the Communists rather than the Anarchists were going to control the future situation in this part of Spain. Helped tremendously by the arrival of Soviet military aid to the Spanish government, the Communists felt themselves in a strong enough position to begin the destruction not only of their Anarchist opponents but also of their own dissident groups.

On 7th December *Pravda* declared: 'So far as Catalonia is concerned, the cleaning up of Trotskyites and Anarchists has begun, and it will be carried out with the same energy as in the U.S.S.R.' It was in December that Orwell arrived in Barcelona.

He came as a journalist but almost immediately joined a militia organized by one of the dissident Trotskyite groups known as P.O.U.M. (Worker-Party of Marxist Unification). 'I myself never joined the party,' he declared, '—for which afterwards, when the P.O.U.M. was suppressed, I was rather sorry.' From January to April he fought as a P.O.U.M. infantryman on the Aragon front ('It was beastly while it was happening, but it is a good patch for my mind to dwell on'). He happened to be on leave in Barcelona when the differences between the Communists and the government on the one hand and the Anarchists and P.O.U.M. on the other materialized into street fighting at the beginning of May. He was wounded at the front a week or two later and left Spain in late June, 1937. He spent the last few days hiding from the police in Barcelona, where the by now Communist-dominated government was beginning to round up the members of the political group with which he had fought. It was the month in which was held the third of the Moscow Purge Trials, at which army leaders were accused of being German agents.

In the early stages of Orwell's Spanish experience the fact that several left-wing groups existed did not seem important. Their differences from one another were apparently cancelled out by their difference from the kind of Spain represented by Franco. He admits that at the start he was unaware of the political situation. The war was vaguely against Fascism and for common decency—the defence of civilization against

> . . . a maniacal outbreak by an army of Colonel Blimps in the pay of Hitler. The revolutionary atmosphere of Barcelona had attracted me deeply, but I had made no attempt to understand it. As for the kaleidoscope of political parties and trade unions, with their tiresome names—P.S.U.C., P.O.U.M., F.A.I., C.N.T., U.G.T., J.C.I., J.S.U., A.I.T.—they merely exasperated me. It looked at first sight as though Spain were suffering from a plague of initials. I knew that I was serving in something called the P.O.U.M. (I had only joined the P.O.U.M. militia rather than any other because I happened to arrive in Barcelona with I.L.P. papers), but I did not realize that there were serious differences between the political parties.   HC 48; P 46

(The I.L.P. is the Independent Labour Party, which was disaffiliated from the Labour Party itself in 1932: the British left-wing had its own troubles.)

Stephen Spender once described the Spanish Civil War as the 1848 of the 20th century. For Orwell it was, as for so many of his contemporaries, a chance to make anti-Fascism something more active than the gesture of joining some Popular Front committee. In fact, over two thousand men from Great Britain fought in Spain, and five hundred of these were killed.

> When the fighting broke out on 18 July it is probable that every anti-Fascist in Europe felt a thrill of hope. For here at last, apparently, was democracy standing up to Fascism. For years past the so-called democratic countries had been surrendering to Fascism at every step. . . . But when Franco tried to overthrow a mildly Left-wing Government the Spanish people, against all expectation, had risen against him. It seemed—possibly it was—the turning of the tide.   HC 49; P 48

Here was the old struggle of oppressed against oppressor, crystallized now in an exotic setting. Auden's poem *Spain* (which Orwell thought was one of the best things written about the war) describes how 'On that arid square . . . Our fever's menacing shapes are precise and alive'. In his essay 'Looking Back on the Spanish War' (1943), Orwell wrote:

> The hatred which the Spanish Republic excited in millionaires, dukes, cardinals, play-boys, Blimps and what-not would in itself be enough to show one how the land lay. In essence it was a class war. If it had been won, the cause of the common people everywhere would have been strengthened. It was lost, and the dividend-drawers all over the world rubbed their hands. That was the real issue; all else was froth on its surface.   EYE 169; COL E 201

The attempt by ordinary people to achieve for themselves the decent life now technically possible was symbolized by the Italian militiaman he momentarily saw in the Lenin Barracks during his first weeks in Barcelona, a 'visual reminder of what the war was really about'. It was this man, the flower of the European working class, harried by the police, filling the mass graves of the Spanish battlefields, rotting in prison camps, who represented the real issue: 'the struggle of the gradually awakening common people against the lords of property and their hired liars and bumsuckers'.

In June 1937 he wrote to Cyril Connolly, whom he had known since their days at the same prep. school: 'I have seen wonderful things and at last really believe in Socialism, which I never did before'. And in the reminiscent essay just referred to he described his months in Spain as 'a time when generous feelings and gestures were easier than they ordinarily were'. Barcelona, a city with the working class in the saddle, and where there were very few well-dressed people, was startling and overwhelming, 'queer and moving':

> There was much in it that I did not understand, in some ways I did not even like it, but I recognized it immediately as a state of affairs worth fighting for. . . . Above all, there was a belief in the revolution and the future, a feeling of having suddenly emerged into an

era of equality and freedom. Human beings were trying to behave as human beings and not as cogs in the capitalist machine.

HC 3; P 9

The militias, having no ranks as they are usually understood, no titles, badges, heel-clicking or saluting, were a microcosm of this new society—all the more so because armies seem fundamentally authoritarian. Life on the front in the Aragon hills west of Barcelona provided a rarefied revolutionary atmosphere: 'one was experiencing a foretaste of socialism'—perfect equality in theory, something not far from it in practice; the disappearance of snobbishness, money-grubbing, fear of the boss—'many of the normal motives of civilized life'; the disappearance of class division 'to an extent that is almost unthinkable in the money-tainted air of England':

> However much one cursed at the time, one realized afterwards that one had been in contact with something strange and valuable. One had been in a community where hope was more normal than apathy or cynicism, where the word 'comrade' stood for comradeship and not, as in most countries, for humbug. One had breathed the air of equality. . . . In that community where no one was on the make, where there was a shortage of everything but no privilege and no boot-licking, one got, perhaps, a crude forecast of what the opening stages of Socialism might be like. And, after all, instead of disillusioning me it deeply attracted me. The effect was to make my desire to see Socialism established much more actual than it had been before.   HC III; P 102

But in a few months the splendour was gone. In Barcelona people had lost interest in the war, the old class distinctions were re-appearing, and by the beginning of May 'there was a perpetual vague sense of danger, a consciousness of some evil thing that was impending', an atmosphere of 'suspicion, hatred, censored newspapers, crammed jails, enormous food queues and prowling gangs of armed men'. On the train coming out of Spain in June, detectives took the names of all foreigners. They were apparently satisfied by Orwell's bourgeois respectability because he was sitting in the dining car: 'It was queer how everything had changed. Only six months ago, when the Anarchists

71

still reigned, it was looking like a proletarian that made you respectable.'

This change was due not so much to the inevitable loss of revolutionary impetus as to a deliberate betrayal of the revolution. The Anarchists no longer reigned because the Communists had eliminated them.

Orwell came to feel that the P.O.U.M. was right to insist that the anti-Fascist war could not be separated from the Socialist revolution, and that the Communists were wrong when they advocated delaying the revolution until after the defeat of Franco. More than this—he believed that the Spanish Communists were deliberately sabotaging the revolution because of their subservience to Stalin's foreign policy. He also believed that Soviet Russia was supplying the government with arms only on anti-revolutionary conditions. The government had to get back whatever power remained in the hands of the trade unions, mainly by use of the 'otherwise we shall lose the war' argument: 'in every case, needless to say, it appeared that the thing demanded by military necessity was the surrender of something that the workers had won for themselves in 1936'. Similarly, the Communists set about the destruction of the egalitarian principles in the P.O.U.M. and Anarchist militias which had made them such breeding grounds of revolutionary ideas.

> The Daily Mail, with its tales of red revolution financed by Moscow, was even more wildly wrong than usual. In reality it was the Communists above all others who prevented revolution in Spain. Later, when the Right-wing forces were in full control, the Communists showed themselves willing to go a great deal further than the Liberals in hunting down the revolutionary leaders.

> HC 59; P 54

One aspect of the betrayal was particularly frightening: the Communist attempt to destroy the historical record. Orwell witnessed certain events: he saw the P.O.U.M. infantrymen dying in the war against Franco; he saw P.O.U.M. militiamen caught up in the street-fighting in Barcelona between the Anarchists and the Communists. Then he read accusations that the P.O.U.M. was a secret Fascist group plotting against the

The demoralizing effect of long unemployment in England in the thirties

Workers marching in protest during the English Depression, 1936

The totalitarian state: members of the German Labour Service marching in front of Hitler, 1937

The devastating effect of a long internment in Belsen Concentration Camp, 1945

revolution, and he saw the men he had been fighting alongside imprisoned as traitors.

The record of what he had seen was being falsified, and the falsification was being accepted as the truth in Popular Front versions of the war. It was Orwell's concern (as it was later to be that of the hero of *Nineteen Eighty-Four*) to try to set down what had really happened—even if this meant spoiling a personal account of fighting in Spain, and reducing what might have been literature to the level of journalism. A squalid brawl in a distant city was more important than appeared at first sight:

> Compared with the huge miseries of a civil war, this kind of inter-necine squabble between parties, with its inevitable injustices and false accusations, may appear trivial. It is not really so. I believe that libels and press-campaigns of this kind, and the habits of mind they indicate, are capable of doing the most deadly damage to the anti-Fascist cause. HC 191; P 170

In April 1938 he wrote to Spender about the controversial parts of the book he had just finished: 'I hate writing that kind of stuff and I am much more interested in my own experiences, but unfortunately in this bloody period we are living in one's only experiences *are* being mixed up in controversies, intrigues etc. I sometimes feel as if I hadn't been properly alive since the beginning of 1937.'

On a fairly elementary level these inter-party polemics meant that various newspaper accounts of any given incident were inconsistent, from which it appeared merely that the left-wing press was as dishonest as the right-wing. On a more sophisticated level it suggested the disappearance of objective, historical truth. At any moment by the manipulation of words a situation could be reversed to suit the changed political landscape. Orwell, in 'Looking Back on the Spanish War', relates how he once said to Arthur Koestler (whose novel *Darkness at Noon* makes passing reference to the possibility of revised editions of newspapers) that history stopped in 1936—'at which he nodded in immediate understanding':

We were both thinking of totalitarianism in general, but more particularly of the Spanish civil war. Early in life I have noticed that no event is ever correctly reported in a newspaper, but in Spain, for the first time, I saw newspaper reports which did not bear any relation to the facts, not even the relationship which is implied in an ordinary lie. . . . I saw, in fact, history being written not in terms of what happened but of what ought to have happened according to various 'party-lines'. . . . This kind of thing is frightening to me, because it often gives me the feeling that the very concept of objective truth is fading out of the world. After all, the chances are that those lies, or at any rate similar lies, will pass into history. . . . The implied objective of this line of thought is a nightmare world in which the Leader, or some ruling clique, controls not only the future but *the past*. If the Leader says of such and such an event, 'It never happened'—well, it never happened. If he says that two and two are five—well, two and two are five. This prospect frightens me much more than bombs—and after our experiences of the last few years that is not a frivolous statement.

EYE 161; COL E 195

That was written during the Second World War, two years before *Animal Farm*, six years before *Nineteen Eighty-Four* in which the problems of doublethink, reality control and the mutability of the past are worked out to their logical conclusions. In 1938 Orwell's final reaction to Spain was not completely pessimistic; the disaster had left mainly evil memories but not necessarily either disillusionment or cynicism: 'Curiously enough the whole experience has left me with not less but more belief in the decency of human beings.'

It is usually claimed that the Spanish Civil War divided intelligent British opinion more than any other foreign event since the French Revolution. It did this because the war could be regarded in so many different ways: Fascism against Communism; totalitarianism against democracy; catholicism against atheism; culture against barbarism; upper class against lower. As Orwell was writing *Homage to Catalonia*, there were major debates on Spain at both the T.U.C. and the Labour Party Conferences in the autumn of 1937, but to him, coming back to the sleek landscape of southern England, what was most alarming was the country's innocence of the processes which were becoming familiar in most other European countries. It was difficult to believe that anything was happening anywhere. There may be earthquakes in Japan and revolutions in Mexico, but in England everybody knew that the milk would be on the doorstep next morning, that the *New Statesman* would appear on Friday. Everybody was still sleeping the deep, deep sleep of England 'from which I sometimes fear that we shall never wake till we are jerked out of it by the roar of bombs'.

'ANIMAL FARM'

In 1947 a Ukrainian translation of *Animal Farm* was published, for which Orwell wrote a preface. In this he described the book's genesis, referring to the purge of the Barcelona P.O.U.M. as a kind of supplement to the Moscow Purge Trials, and stating his belief, after the summer of 1937, that before there could be any revival of European Socialism the myth of Soviet justice and infallibility under Stalin would have to be exploded.

Animal Farm itself was written during the winter of 1943–44, and many publishers apparently felt the time to be unsuitable for such an explosion: the Battle for Stalingrad (the major turning-point of the war) had been won by January 1943, and the Red Army entered Berlin in April 1945. Before the book was accepted Orwell had thought of publishing it privately, with an introductory essay on the freedom of the press. He believed that the anti-Stalinist line of *Homage to Catalonia* had made many of the literary intellectuals hostile to him.

In the idea of a revolution carried out by farm animals Orwell found a kind of extended metaphor (technically, a fable) by which he could embody his first-hand experience of Spain and what he had read about Soviet Russia, and by which he could symbolize the tyrannous possibilities inherent in any revolutionary seizure of power. It was, he wrote, 'the first book in which I tried, with full consciousness of what I was doing, to fuse political purpose and artistic purpose into one whole'. It was an attempt to create a piece of that 'concentration camp literature' which he felt an over-sheltered England needed to read.

75

Under the incapable régime of the human farmer, Jones, the animals are shown by Major, the philosopher of the revolution, that their lives are ignorant of happiness and leisure, and are miserably enslaved, laborious and short. And they are so not because it is in their nature, but because the animals are the victims of exploiters:

'Is it not crystal clear, then, comrades, that all the evils of this life of ours spring from the tyranny of human beings? Only get rid of Man, and the produce of our labour would be our own. Almost overnight we could become rich and free. What then must we do? Why, work night and day, body and soul, for the overthrow of the human race! . . . And remember, comrades, your resolution must never falter. No argument must lead you astray. Never listen when they tell you that Man and the animals have a common interest, that the prosperity of the one is the prosperity of the others. It is all lies. Man serves the interests of no creature except himself. And among us animals let there be perfect unity, perfect comradeship in the struggle. All men are enemies. All animals are comrades. . . . And remember also that in fighting against Man, we must not come to resemble him. Even when you have conquered him, do not adopt his vices. . . . All the habits of Man are evil. And, above all, no animal must ever tyrannize over his own kind. Weak or strong, clever or simple, we are all brothers. No animal must ever kill any other animal. All animals are equal.'   AF 9; P 10

Some day, when man the exploiter and expropriator is himself expropriated, a golden future time will come when the fruitful fields of England are trodden by beasts alone:

Bright will shine the fields of England,
Purer shall its waters be,
Sweeter yet shall blow its breezes
On the day that sets us free.   AF 12; P 13

After the spontaneous uprising of the animals, the hurried departure of Jones and his wife, and the destruction of the old instruments of oppression kept in the harness room, it seems as if Major's Utopian dream has come true. In the spring dawn the animals survey the farm:

Yes, it was theirs—everything that they could see was theirs! In the ecstasy of that thought they gambolled round and round, they hurled themselves into the air in great leaps of excitement. They rolled in the dew, they cropped mouthfuls of the sweet summer grass, they kicked up clods of the black earth and snuffed its rich scent. Then they made a tour of inspection of the whole farm. . . . It was as though they had never seen these things before, and even now they could hardly believe that it was all their own.

AF 19; P 21

It is the job of the rest of the book to illustrate the destruction of the attitudes and excitement behind this rejoicing, which is repeated in the happiness of bringing in the first harvest when everyone works according to his capacity, and more efficiently than the humans. Nobody steals; nobody grumbles: 'the quarrelling and biting and jealousy which had been normal features of life in the old days had almost disappeared.'

This destruction is most of all suggested by the piecemeal alteration of the Commandments—collectively that 'unalterable law by which all animals on Animal Farm must live forever after' which is summarized in the slogan: 'Four legs good, two legs bad.'

The pigs, having learnt to read, immediately emerge as what sociologists call a power élite. They are the only ones able to put forward resolutions at the weekly policy-debates (while such debates continue); they are the organizers of the various animal committees; they are the ones who declare they must govern if Jones is not to return. And to govern seems to require privilege. At first this is trivial. The pigs get milk in their mash; they get all the apples; they move into the farmhouse which it had originally been resolved should become a museum; they rise later than the other animals. Then it becomes less trivial. The pigs do not work but bureaucratically supervise the work of others; they and the dogs seem to be the only animals to benefit from the farm's increasing prosperity. Then it is so un-trivial as to represent a fundamental betrayal of the revolution. The pigs walk upright and carry whips; the slogan becomes: 'Four legs good, two legs better.'

Within this élite there is the expected struggle for leadership: there are stormy debates between Napoleon and Snowball over the farm's sowing policy, over the question of whether the farm should concentrate on self-defence or on exporting the revolution to neighbouring farms, over the building of the windmill. The struggle is decided by Napoleon's possession of the savage dogs which wag their tails to him as their predecessors used to do to Mr. Jones, and which finally chase Snowball off the farm. Once this has happened, and the leader has become a further élite of one within the élite itself, the familiar pattern emerges.

There is the kind of adulation of Napoleon which—after the deaths of both Orwell and Stalin—came to be known as the 'personality cult':

> Napoleon was now never spoken of simply as 'Napoleon'. He was always referred to in formal style as 'our Leader, Comrade Napoleon', and the pigs liked to invent for him such titles as Father of All Animals, Terror of Mankind, Protector of the Sheep-fold, Ducklings' Friend. . . . It had become usual to give Napoleon the credit for every successful achievement and every stroke of good fortune. You would often hear one hen remark to another, 'Under the guidance of our Leader, Comrade Napoleon, I have laid five eggs in six days'; or two cows, enjoying a drink at the pool, would exclaim, 'Thanks to the leadership of Comrade Napoleon, how excellent this water tastes!' AF 72; P 79

There are the complete reversals of the Party-line—for example, over the building of the windmill, or over the selling of the timber to Frederick or Pilkington. There is the modification of 'truth' to fit such alterations: Napoleon had only pretended to oppose the building of the mill as a tactic to get rid of Snowball who was a bad influence—and who in any case had originally stolen the plans from Napoleon's own papers. Nor had Snowball really led the animals to victory at the Battle of the Cowshed; in fact he had been Jones's secret agent.

Fictitious production figures reeled off by Squealer, food bins filled with sand and topped off with meal, ritual designed to distract attention from empty bellies—it is a society well on the way to the 'reality-control' of Oceania and 1984. Yet things must be better than they were in the old days of the unjust society; memories in any case were fading. Now life was harsh and bare; the animals were often hungry and cold, usually working when not asleep. But whereas in the past they had been slaves, they were now free, 'and that made all the difference, as Squealer did not fail to point out'.

The end is a community constructed not only on lies but also on terror—like the Barcelona of those summer months in 1937. The consummating act of the Revolution, according to Squealer, is the massacre (after their confessions) of all oppositional elements —the pigs who had protested against the discontinuation of the meetings at which policy could be debated, the hens who had led a rebellion over the sale of their eggs to the humans, the sheep who had urinated in the drinking pool. There is a pile of corpses at Napoleon's feet 'and the air was heavy with the smell of blood which had been unknown there since the expulsion of Jones'. A melancholy spring evening balances the joyous summer morning experienced by the animals at the start of their revolutionary society:

> Never had the farm—and with a kind of surprise they remembered that it was their own farm, every inch of it their own property— appeared to the animals so desirable a place. As Clover looked down the hillside her eyes filled with tears. If she could have spoken her thoughts, it would have been to say that this was not what they had aimed at when they had set themselves years ago to work for the overthrow of the human race. These scenes of terror and slaughter were not what they had looked forward to on that night when old Major first stirred them to rebellion. If she herself had had any picture of the future, it had been of a society of animals set free from hunger and the whip, all equal, each working according to his capacity, the strong protecting the weak. . . . Instead—she did not know why—they had come to a time when no one dared speak his mind, when fierce, growling dogs roamed everywhere, and when you had to watch your comrades torn to pieces after confessing to shocking crimes.

AF 68; P 75

'Beasts of England', the song that proclaimed liberty, is replaced by 'Animal Farm, Animal Farm, Never through me shalt thou come to harm', a song that proclaims only loyalty. Yet even an almost unquestioning loyalty is betrayed. Boxer, with his slogans of 'I will work harder' and 'Napoleon is always right', ends up at the knacker's as soon as his strength is exhausted, and so fulfils Major's prophecy of what would happen to him under the régime of the humans.

The pigs have become 'the new class' (the phrase is that of Milovan Djilas, a leading Yugoslav Communist, imprisoned by Tito because of his political unorthodoxy). Their children are isolated from the rest of the community, brought up and educated as an hereditary élite. In fact the pigs have become far more efficient exploiters of the other animals than ever Jones was, and other human farmers come to learn from them the new techniques. Having denied the bringer of the original revolutionary message, having changed the name of the farm back to its 'correct' pre-revolutionary one, having suppressed the 'foolish custom' the animals had of calling one another 'comrade', the pigs in their duplicity become physically identical with the human beings they are entertaining.

Orwell subtitled his book 'A Fairy Story'—a thing that had proved to be a disappointing illusion. This, to many people in the West, was what one of the potentially greatest experiments in political engineering ever undertaken had turned into, as the Russia of the 1917 Revolution had changed into the Stalinist Russia of the thirties and forties. One of the best-known accounts of the sense of betrayal this change caused in European intellectuals like Koestler, Silone, Gide and Spender is called *The God That Failed* (it was published in 1950, after Orwell's death).

It is possible to read into *Animal Farm* very close parallels with the course of Soviet history between 1917 and, say, 1945. Thus Napoleon would represent Stalin, and Snowball Trotsky, whose quarrel with Stalin after Lenin's death in 1924 led to his expulsion from the Party and from Russia itself (in 1929). Trotsky's leading role in the 1917 October Bolshevik rising and in the Civil War has been 'revalued' by Soviet historians just as Snowball's military leadership was revalued by the pigs. Molly would represent those Russians who fled the country after 1917; Boxer would represent the faithful proletariat; Moses the raven would represent the Russian Orthodox Church. Similarly the Battle of the Cowshed would represent the Civil War that followed the Revolution (Jones is helped by men from the neighbouring farms of Foxwood and Pinchfield; some western countries sent troops to help the White Russian forces); the Battle of the Windmill would be the German invasion of 1941. The building of the windmill would be the industrialization of Russia—a policy taken over by Stalin from Trotsky, after he had originally opposed it.

It is possible to see connections in quite small details: for example, the fact that two sheep confess to having murdered a devoted follower of Napoleon by chasing him round a bonfire when he had a cough presumably refers to the accusation, which emerged at the Moscow Purge Trials, that the death of the Russian novelist Gorki had been accelerated when certain anti-revolutionary elements lighted a fire under his bedroom window. The horn-and-hoof flag, the adulatory references to Napoleon, the statistics always given as a percentage of a base figure which is unknown—all these are part of the atmosphere of Stalinist Russia.

But two things are important. This book is not an allegory in which everything has to stand for something else. To read it in this way reduces it to the level of a sophisticated crossword puzzle. Thus there is no figure corresponding to Lenin (Major dies before the rising takes place); and the farm does take on a life of its own. The friendship between Clover and Boxer, or the cynicism of Benjamin do not need to be explained in terms of actual history. It may be that, for those who know their history, the rebellion of the hens seems parallel to the rebellion of the Russian sailors at Kronstadt in 1921, or that the two farmers Frederick and Pilkington represent Germany and England. But it is not really necessary to an understanding of the book (and may lead to incorrect history) to work at this level of detail.

Indeed by doing so, you may miss the wider implications of Orwell's fairy-tale. Napoleon is presumably not given that name by accident, and the Russian Revolution is not the only one to have ended in dictatorship. If you read the relevant parts of

The Prelude you will find there Wordsworth's own story of another god that failed when the movement that started with the fall of the Bastille ended in the Jacobin terror. (When we now read, in the first book of *Gulliver's Travels*, that Flimnap the Treasurer can cut a caper on the tightrope higher than any one else we can learn from the notes that a reference to Walpole is intended; but it seems to be a pity to limit the parallel between holding office and ability to dance on a rope to a politician who died over two hundred years ago.) *Animal Farm* was apparently serialized some years ago in an opposition newspaper in Ghana under the Nkrumah régime, and for its readers then Napoleon presumably took on another, more local identity.

'All animals are equal, but some animals are more equal than others' is the most famous sentence Orwell ever wrote. It says something about human beings and their history, particularly in the 20th century. It says something about the Russian Revolution because that event is a part—perhaps the central part—of that 20th-century history.

5

Five Characters and Their Worlds

THE CRYSTAL SPIRIT

Trying to convey the 'ideal to be striven after' as it is shown in
Dickens's novels, Orwell gives the following picture of the kind
of Christmas atmosphere—purposeless but full of a tremendous
vitality—which is at the centre of what has come to be known
as 'the Dickens world', and which provides the note on which
many of the novels end:

> . . . a hundred thousand pounds, a quaint old house with plenty of
> ivy on it, a sweetly womanly wife, a horde of children, and no work.
> Everything is safe, soft, peaceful and, above all, domestic . . . the
> children prattle round your feet, the old friends sit at your fireside,
> talking of past days, there is the endless succession of enormous
> meals, the cold punch and sherry negus, the feather beds and warm-
> ing-pans, the Christmas parties with charades and blind man's buff;
> but nothing ever happens, except the yearly childbirth. The curious
> thing is that it is a genuinely happy picture. . . . CE 44; COL E 72

Orwell's own novels (there are five of them, if we exclude
Animal Farm) suggest a very different atmosphere. This is much
nearer to that of another writer he admired—George Gissing.
Gissing, according to Orwell, was the chronicler of vulgarity,
squalor and failure. His novels protested against the form of
self-torture known as English respectability, and analysed the way
in which respectability's two agents, money and women, were
used by society to avenge itself on a courage and intellect that
tried to go its own way.

In an essay called 'Benefit of Clergy' where he discusses the
autobiography of the Spanish surrealist painter Salvador Dali,
Orwell wrote that any man who gave a good account of himself

83

was probably lying 'since any life when viewed from the inside is simply a series of defeats'. Physically such defeat came to the Italian militiaman who symbolized for Orwell the flower of the oppressed European working class, and whom he so briefly saw in the Barcelona barracks during the Spanish Civil War:

> Your name and your deeds were forgotten
> Before your bones were dry,
> And the lie that slew you is buried
> Under a deeper lie.

Such physical annihilation did not mean spiritual destruction. A man's humanness, his crystal spirit, his integrity, may stand out all the clearer because he has been prepared to run the risk of being killed when fighting for it:

> But the thing that I saw in your face
> No power can disinherit:
> No bomb that ever burst
> Shatters the crystal spirit.   EYE 176; COL E 208

However, the sequence of Orwell's novels ends at just such a shattering of the spirit, a complete disinheritance from one's birthright as a human being, a final destruction of the attempt to carry on the human tradition. It could perhaps be argued that Flory avoids further defeat and loneliness by committing suicide; that Dorothy Hare has learnt to face a future of penury, spinster-hood and disbelief; that Comstock can be satisfied with life as a successful ad-man, forgetting the defeat of his revolt against respectable money-making; that Bowling can accept the destruction of his dream-world, and live on as a suburban, wife-nagged insurance-salesman in a civilization that has become a gigantic dustbin. The crystal spirit takes some fairly hard knocks in all their cases—but there can be little doubt of its complete shattering in the case of Winston Smith, as he sits in the Chestnut Tree Café, sipping his Victory Gin and loving Big Brother.

In the first-published of the novels, *Burmese Days*, Orwell makes the hero use a fairly trivial metaphor to express his longing for a world he can accept and which will accept him:

'One should live with the stream of life, not against it.' The same metaphor occurs in the last-published novel, *Nineteen Eighty-Four*, when Smith, in the cells of the Ministry of Love, has almost brought himself to believe that two and two can make five. It was a question of surrendering: you had been swimming against a current that swept you back however hard you struggled; then you decided 'to turn round and go with the current instead of opposing it'. Orwell's protagonists are characters who for various reasons cannot swim in the stream as it flows in their own societies. Their stories are records of their attempts to make a few strokes in another direction—and wherever those strokes lead, it is far away from the cosy Christmas domesticity where everyone is genuinely happy and swimming alongside everybody else.

In the following presentation the five novels—or rather the activities of their central characters—are treated in their order of publication.

JOHN FLORY, 'BURMESE DAYS', 1934

In the middle of the nineteen-twenties Flory is a thirty-five-year-old teak-extractor who both loves and hates Burma. He longs for someone with whom he can share interests and memories, and with whom he can escape from the smell of pukka-sahibdom. He hates himself for the cowardice of admitting, after fifteen years in the country, that it is unwise to oppose public opinion. He constantly manœuvres to keep out of sight the disfiguring birthmark which at school earned him the nickname of Monkeybum. He drifts 'rotting in dishonour and horrible futility, and all the while knowing that somewhere within one there is the possibility of a decent human being'.

To his fellow Anglo-Indians Flory seems to let the side down, mainly because of an unsound attitude to the natives. To himself he seems to be living in a poisonous hatred of imperialism and its life of lies:

Year after year you sit in Kipling-haunted little Clubs, whisky to right of you, *Pink'un* to left of you, listening and eagerly agreeing while Colonel Bodger develops his theory that these bloody Nationalists should be boiled in oil. You hear your Oriental friends called 'greasy little babus,' and you admit, dutifully, that they *are* greasy little babus. You see louts fresh from school kicking grey-haired servants. The time comes when you burn with hatred of your own countrymen, when you long for a native rising to drown their Empire in blood . . . . each year Flory found himsel less at home in the world of the sahibs, more liable to get into trouble when he talked seriously on any subject whatever. So he had learned to live inwardly, secretly, in books and secret thoughts that could not be uttered. BD 69; P 66

When not working in the jungle he idles at the European Club, 'the spiritual citadel, the real seat of the British power, the Nirvana for which native officials and millionaires pine in vain'. Here gather his colleagues to drink, play bridge, gossip, read *Punch*, *The Field* or *La Vie Parisienne*, and wait until the conversation veers round to the usual subjects—'. . . the insolence of the natives, the supineness of the Government, the dear dead days, when the British Raj *was* the British Raj and please give the bearer fifteen lashes'.

Here are such people as Macgregor ('He had no prejudice against Orientals; indeed he was deeply fond of them. Provided they were given no freedom he thought them the most charming people alive'); Westfield, permanently regretting he can't clear the air by shooting a few dozen ('It's all this law and order that's done for us'); Mrs. Lackersteen ('We seem to have no *authority* over the natives nowadays, with all these dreadful Reforms, and the insolence they learn from the newspapers. In some ways they are getting as bad as the lower classes at Home'); and Ellis ('Here we are, supposed to be governing a set of damn black swine who've been slaves since the beginning of history, and instead of ruling them in the only way they understand, we go and treat them as equals').

It is Ellis who gives most vivid expression to the Club's racialism when official policy suggests the expediency of admitting at least one native member. This is a critical moment, and the natives must be treated firmly as the dirt they are. Since to

Ellis any suggestion of friendship with an Oriental seems a horrible perversity, and since Flory maintains one such friendship, he becomes the main target:

> 'My God, I should have thought in a case like this, when it's a question of keeping those black, stinking swine out of the only place where we can enjoy ourselves, you'd have the decency to back me up. Even if that pot-bellied, greasy little sod of a nigger doctor *is* your best pal. *I* don't care if you choose to pal up with the scum of the bazaar. If it pleases you to go to Veraswami's house and drink whisky with all his nigger pals, that's your look-out. Do what you like outside the Club. But, by God, it's a different matter when you talk of bringing niggers in here.'   BD 23; P 22

Before he starts throwing bottles and smashing pictures, Flory has to escape from the society of 'dull boozing witless porkers' repeating the same evil-minded drivel week after week.

> Oh, what a place, what people! What a civilization is this of ours —this godless civilization founded on whisky, *Blackwood's* and the 'Bonzo' pictures! God have mercy on us, for all of us are part of it.
> BD 33; P 31

He finds relief from 'them' ('my beloved fellow Empire-builders. British prestige, the white man's burden, the pukka sahib sans peur et sans reproche') by seditious talk with Veraswami, the Indian doctor who is the only friend he has made during his years in Burma. But even this friend he later betrays by signing Ellis's statement that club-members are against the introduction of any native element: 'The doctor was a good fellow, but as to championing him against the full fury of pukka-sahibdom—ah, no, no! What shall it profit a man if he save his own soul and lose the whole world?'

To Veraswami, more in love with the English than they are with themselves, the Empire-building sahibs are the torchbearers upon the path of progress, gloriously loyal, full of the Public School Spirit, some admittedly arrogant but even then possessing sterling qualities lacked by Orientals. Above all they are modernizers, destroyers of the dirt, torture and ignorance of the Burmese past. Flory, on the contrary, prefers things 'a bit septic'.

The English are not civilizing the Burmese, but merely rubbing dirt on to them. 'Modernization' will only lead

> ... to our own dear old swinery of gramophones and billycock hats. Sometimes I think that in two hundred years all this . . . will be gone—forests, villages, monasteries, pagodas all vanished. And instead, pink villas fifty yards apart; all over those hills, as far as you can see, villa after villa, with all the gramophones playing the same tune. And all the forests shaved flat—chewed into wood-pulp for the *News of the World*, or sawn up into gramophone cases.

> BD 42; P 40

Veraswami needs Flory's support against the intriguing of a native sub-divisional magistrate; thus the Englishman is on the verge of breaking another of the sahibs' precepts: never entangle yourself with native quarrels. 'With Indians there must be no loyalty, no real friendship. Affection, even love—yes. . . . But alliance, partisanship, never! Even to know the rights and wrongs of a "native" quarrel is a loss of prestige.'

Into this society comes Elizabeth Lackersteen, now orphaned and penniless, but once having briefly rubbed shoulders with the rich at a school where four of the girls were 'the Honourable'. It was an experience which fixed her character for life: the Good (or 'lovely') was synonymous with the Expensive, the Elegant, the Aristocratic; the Bad (or 'beastly') was synonymous with the Cheap, the Shabby, the Laborious.

Because her mother had once gone to seed playing at being an artist in Paris, Elizabeth loathes art. Her best Parisian moments are spent in the American Library scanning the *Sketch*, the *Tatler* or the *Graphic*, where she can find evidence of the golden world to which for two terms she had belonged, a world in which 'braininess' can be regarded as another aspect of the beastly. Here lived the real people, shooting grouse, yachting at Cowes, going to Ascot—not going in for writing books and fooling round with paint-brushes 'and all these highbrow ideas—Socialism and all that. "Highbrow" was a bitter word in her vocabulary'.

She has to find a husband if she is to be rescued from further beastliness, and Ellis, with a characteristic simile, warns Flory that he is the prospective victim: 'The Indian marriage market, they call it. Meat market it ought to be. Shiploads of 'em coming out every year like carcasses of frozen mutton to be pawed over by nasty old bachelors like you.'

The relationship between the two develops uneasily against a background of growing trouble. From the first she feels doubtful about his attempts to interest her in native Burma, and she is made uncomfortable by his flood of nervous talk in which she suspects hearing more than once the word 'art'. Her reaction to a native dance ('Why had he brought her here, among this horde of natives, to watch this hideous and savage spectacle?') is to leave just as a dancer has been brought on especially in her honour; this was not how white men ought to behave:

> And that extraordinary rambling speech that he had begun with all those long words—almost, she thought bitterly, as though he were quoting poetry! BD 107; P 102

It is the same in the bazaar where she retreats in disgust from a Chinese tea-shop, or when she snubs the Eurasians with whom Flory talks, trying, when he has the pluck, not to be a pukka sahib. They meet every day for tennis, bridge and conversation, yet he can never be at ease with her. As far as he is concerned, she has changed the orbit of his mind, bringing the air of England 'where thought is free and one is not condemned forever to dance the danse du pukka sahib for the edification of the lower races'. But he can't make her respond:

> They talked—so long as they talked of trivialities—with the utmost freedom, yet they were distant, like strangers. . . . For somehow, he had never been able to talk to her as he longed to talk. To talk, simply to talk! It sounds so little, and how much it is! When you have existed to the brink of middle age in bitter loneliness, among people to whom your true opinion on every subject on earth is blasphemy, the need to talk is the greatest of all needs. Yet with Elizabeth serious talk seemed impossible. It was as though there had been a spell upon them that made all their conversation lapse into banality; gramophone records, dogs, tennis racquets—all that desolating Club-chatter. She seemed not to *want* to talk of anything but that. He had only to touch upon a subject of any conceivable

89

interest to hear the evasion, the 'I shan't play', coming into her voice.   BD 116; P 111

Spiritually she is as far from him as is Ellis; his striving to interest her in Oriental things strikes her as perverse—'a deliberate seeking after the squalid and the "beastly" '. At each of his attempts to make her share his life, thoughts and sense of beauty, she shies away like a frightened horse.

Only once, when he is talking of tiger-shooting ('If only he would always talk about shooting, instead of about books and Art and that mucky poetry'), does she really warm to him. And it is immediately after a tiger-shoot, with the scales finally turned in Flory's favour by the fact that Elizabeth's uncle has started trying to make love to her, that she decides to accept him. But even as Flory kisses her before his formal proposal, he smells the scent of a frangipani tree which seems to symbolize his exile and the gulf between them: 'How should he ever make her understand what it was that he wanted of her?'

His last effort to explain his loneliness fails:

> 'Have I made myself at all clear to you? Have you got some picture of the life we live here? The foreignness, the solitude, the melancholy! Foreign trees, foreign flowers, foreign landscapes, foreign faces. It's all as alien as a different planet. But do you see—and it's this that I so want you to understand—do you see, it mightn't be so bad living on a different planet, it might even be the most interesting thing imaginable, if you had even one person to share it with. One person who could see it with eyes something like your own. This country's been a kind of solitary hell to me—it's so to most of us—and yet I tell you it could be a paradise if one weren't alone. Does all this seem quite meaningless?'   BD 180; P 170

From the few words she has understood she thinks he is talking about an ailment that will disappear when the new portable radio sets arrive in Burma. Before Flory can get to his proposal there is the distraction of a minor earthquake, but—more fatal to his hopes—it is also discovered that a new police official in the town is 'the Honourable', and thus a very superior bargain in the marriage market.

The superior bargain's main concerns are horses and physical health: 'He took no interest in Indians, and his Urdu consisted mainly of swear-words, with all verbs in the third person singular'. To Elizabeth he represents the longed-for world of the rich—romance, the panache of the cavalryman's life, the North-west Frontier, poised lances, regimental messes, gorgeous uniforms: 'How splendid it was, that equestrian world, how splendid! And it was *her* world, she belonged to it, she had been born for it.'

Flory, snubbed and back at work in the jungle, is self-pityingly obsessed by the vision of her in someone else's arms; his earlier sentimental love is replaced by physical longing—a longing not destroyed by his realization of her silliness, snobbishness and heartlessness.

The snub is modified after a local rising in which Flory becomes the hero of the moment, and his happiness increases as he persuades himself that Elizabeth's affair will come to an end when 'the Honourable' has ceased to find it amusing. Thus after the latter's hasty departure (whether to avoid Elizabeth or his creditors is never discovered) the future seems clear. At a Sunday morning service Flory envisages his married life:

> What fun they would have together in this alien yet kindly land! He saw Elizabeth in his camp, greeting him as he came home tired from work . . . he saw her walking in the forest with him. . . . He saw his home as she would remake it. . . . He was delivered for ever from the sub-life of the past decade—the debaucheries, the lies, the pain of exile and solitude, the dealings with whores and money lenders and pukka sahibs.   BD 272; P 257

But Flory's Burmese ex-mistress, acting as part of a local intrigue against him, denounces him during the course of the service. There is no forgiveness from Elizabeth: 'She knew only that he was dishonoured and less than a man, and that she hated him as she would have hated a leper or a lunatic.' For Flory a return to the old sub-life is impossible:

> No, it was not endurable any longer. Since Elizabeth's coming the power to suffer and above all to hope, which he had thought dead in him, had sprung to new life. The half-comfortable lethargy in which he had lived was broken. And if he suffered now, there

was far worse to come. In a little while someone else would marry her.   BD 279; P 265

He returns to his house, shoots his dog, and then himself.

DOROTHY HARE, 'A CLERGYMAN'S DAUGHTER', 1935

Dorothy Hare is the only daughter of a Suffolk clergyman. At the beginning of the nineteen-thirties she lives, aged twenty-seven, in a rectory of shabby gentility. On the walls of the dining-room, itself apparently furnished from the sweepings of an antique shop, are once-valuable engravings ruined by damp. On the breakfast table a silver dish which is an heirloom lies alongside crockery bought at Woolworth's. The church itself is similarly in decay: the belfry floor splintering under the weight of the disused bells which one day must fall through into the porch beneath, the broken pews, the choked stove-flue, the choir-boys' ragged cassocks.

The rector, steadily losing money through bad investments, is unable to understand the need to pay tradesmen's bills. His temper has been incurably soured by marriage. He has quarrelled with all his colleagues, and over a period of twenty-three years has reduced his congregation from six hundred to under two hundred. He is an anachronism in the modern world of Lenin and the *Daily Mail*, chronically exasperated, and working that exasperation off on the person nearest to him—his daughter.

Against this background, Dorothy, regarded by her father as an unpaid curate, steadily works a seventeen-hour day at 'parish duties': distributing the magazine; taking medicine to parishioners; running the Mothers' Union; typing her father's sermons; making costumes for the stream of plays and pageants required for fund-raising. There is a constant struggle to keep the peas free from bindweed, a constant battle against disbelief, a constant round of visiting; gossiping with over-worked housewives, helping with the mending, looking after 'bad legs', playing with sour-smelling children, suggesting names for babies. And it is all profoundly discouraging work:

> Few, very few, of the women seemed to have even a conception of the Christian life that she was trying to help them to lead. ... Yes, it

> was discouraging work; so discouraging that at times it would have
> seemed altogether futile if she had not known the sense of futility for
> what it is—the subtlest weapon of the Devil.   CD 57; P 47

Dorothy's mental life revolves round three problems: material, psychological and spiritual. The material problem is that of money. She has three-pounds-nineteen-and-fourpence left as housekeeping for the next thirty-nine days, and a father 'never so unmoved as when you were reminding him that he was up to his eyes in debt'. The psychological problem (exacerbated by her friendship with Warburton, a local lecher and mediocre artist who sees her as an object for an exercise in seduction) is that of her sexual frigidity. However much she enjoys talking to the man, regarding her infrequent visits to his house as among her few interesting experiences, she is repelled by his physical approaches: 'It was her especial secret, the especial, incurable disability that she carried through life'. The spiritual problem is that in this environment even her instinctive religious belief has to be frustrated because it seems to partake of a heresy often defined by her father. One hot August day she breathes in the scent of fennel, and feels a mystical joy in the beauty of the earth which leads her to prayer. She then finds that she is actually kissing the fennel, and checks herself:

> What was she doing? Was it God that she was worshipping, or was it only the earth? The joy ebbed out of her heart, to be succeeded by the cold, uncomfortable feeling that she had been betrayed into a half-pagan ecstasy. She admonished herself. None of *that*, Dorothy! No Nature-worship, please!   CD 65; P 54

A sudden loss of memory brings escape from all these pressures. Finding herself a week later in London, still not knowing who she is, she joins a group tramping to find work in the Kentish hop-fields. She can find no opportunity to puzzle out either her identity or her past. Even five minutes' consecutive thought is impossible in a dirty sub-world of nightmare—'a nightmare not of urgent terrors, but of hunger, squalor, and fatigue, and alternating heat and cold'. She takes the new life for granted, barely aware that something in the past has been different from this. The hop-picking itself means whole days in the field doing stupid, exhausting, mechanical work; an uneasy five-hour slumber at night; everlasting hunger and the calculation of farthings; a narrowing range of consciousness. 'Your wits seemed to thicken, just as your skin did, in the rain and sunshine and perpetual fresh air.'

This nightmare ends with the return of memory, and the future becomes a matter for fear and doubt. She feels unable to return to face the scandalous gossip that she has really eloped with Warburton, and decides to lose herself, when the picking is over, in London 'where nobody knew her and the mere sight of her face or mention of her name would not drag into the light a string of dirty memories'. Nor can there be any return to the old world of work, and to the prayer which had been the centre of that world:

> In trouble or in happiness, it was to prayer that she had turned. And she realized—the first time that it had crossed her mind—that she had not uttered a prayer since leaving home, not even since her memory had come back to her. Moreover, she was aware that she no longer had the smallest impulse to pray. Mechanically, she began a whispered prayer, and stopped almost instantly; the words were empty and futile. CD 152; P 125

She spends a week in London, searching vainly for a job from her base in a prostitutes' lodging house. Then she gives up and sinks into another manifestation of the sub-world, her earlier panic giving way to apathy: 'there was a night in the streets ahead of her, that was all she knew, and even about that she only vaguely cared.' This is the down-and-out world of Trafalgar Square: the nights spent trying to sleep wrapped in newspaper, lying as part of a human pyramid, disturbed every few hours by the police, waiting for the opening of a café at five in the morning when four people can have the comparative comfort of sitting down to share a halfpenny cup of tea.

From this experience Dorothy is rescued by a rich cousin, through whose help she exchanges the world of Trafalgar Square for that of Mrs. Creevy's Ringwood Academy for Girls in the South-London suburbs—a world governed by the Eleventh Commandment: 'Thou shalt not lose thy job.' Mrs.

Creevy is hard and angular, with 'something discoloured about her whole appearance, as though she lived all her life in a bad light'. She has never completely read a book; her house is cold and uncomfortable; she never does any of the things that ordinary people do to amuse themselves. Christmas is nonsense got up by shopkeepers, and an unnecessary expense; her inexhaustible sources of pleasure are her avarice and her purposeless malignity. Most of her time is spent collecting fees, which are the sole reason for the school's existence—as she explains when disabusing Dorothy of 'all this stuff about developing the children's minds':

> 'After all, it's no more than common sense. It's not to be supposed as anyone'd go to all the trouble of keeping school and having the house turned upside down by a pack of brats, if it wasn't that there's a bit of money to be made out of it.' CD 255; P 208

Thus the twenty-one girls who play chicks to Mrs. Creevy's hawk are divided into good payers (never to be smacked), medium payers (smackable, but not so as to leave a mark), and bad payers (any violence short of causing a police case). The curriculum is largely handwriting and simple arithmetic, geography (lists of capitals), history (British victories) and literature (the reading books are old but good enough for a pack of children). The marks are carefully arranged so that every girl's report shows her near the top.

The children really know nothing. Everything they are taught is aimed at their parents, as are all other aspects of the school (Mrs. Creevy is worried by what her non-conformist clients will make of a Church of England teacher, particularly after an earlier scare when a mistress turned out to be a Roman Catholic). Dorothy's pity for the children and her effort to turn the school 'from a place of bondage into a place human and decent' give her, after a few weeks, a new sense of mission:

> The complex, never-ended labour of teaching filled her life just as the round of parish jobs had filled it at home. She thought and dreamed of teaching; she took books out of the public library and studied theories of education. She felt that quite willingly she would go on teaching all her life, even at ten shillings a week and

her keep, if it could always be like this. It was her vocation, she thought. CD 245; P 200

Geography becomes map-making, history the production of an illustrated wall-chart, literature the reading of *Macbeth*—until the parents discover that this contains obscenities like 'womb'. At the subsequent meeting where Dorothy has to encounter these outraged people, she is told by one of them: 'We don't send our children to school to have ideas put into their heads. I'm speaking for all the parents in saying this.' The result is a return to arithmetic, handwriting and list-learning with a now rebellious class.

Opposed to this greed, dishonesty and brutality there is Dorothy's experience of Sunday morning in church, where she can find a refuge of decency even in a ritual made meaningless by the vanishing of her faith:

> But however little the church services might mean to her, she did not regret the hours she spent in church. On the contrary, she looked forward to her Sunday mornings as blessed interludes of peace; and that not only because Sunday morning meant a respite from Mrs. Creevy's prying eye and nagging voice. In another and deeper sense the atmosphere of the church was soothing and reassuring to her. For she perceived that in all that happens in church, however absurd and cowardly its supposed purpose may be, there is something—it is hard to define, but something of decency, of spiritual comeliness—that is not easily found in the world outside. It seemed to her that even though you no longer believe, it is better to go to church than not; better to follow in the ancient ways, than to drift in rootless freedom. CD 269; P 220

Rescued from her loneliness and 'the corrupting ennui that lies in wait for every modern soul' by being sacked, she is taken back home, her name cleared. But in some ways a return is impossible; in previous years, spring would have meant gratitude to God for a reviving year, but now there was no God to thank, 'and nothing—not a flower or a stone or a blade of grass— nothing in the universe would ever be the same again'.

She renews her acquaintance with Warburton, but he cannot realize 'how a mind naturally pious must recoil from a world discovered to be meaningless'. He cannot see how it may be better and less selfish to go on pretending to believe when real belief fails, and you can find nothing to put in its place. He can only see her future, ten years on, as that of a desperate, worn-out virgin, a derelict parson's daughter without money, profession, or a chance of marrying. She will have to work as a governess or a companion or a school teacher. 'And all the time withering, drying up, growing more sour and more angular and more friendless.'

Even to avoid this she cannot bring herself to marry him. She can only go back to the life that seemed to be hers, but which she cannot explain:

> What she would have said was that though her faith had left her, she had not changed, could not change, did not want to change, the spiritual background of her mind; that her cosmos, though now it seemed to her empty and meaningless, was still in a sense the Christian cosmos; that the Christian way of life was still the way that must come naturally to her.   CD 308; P 252

This woman, just old enough to enter the ranks of the Old Maids of England, understanding that the life of poverty and drudgery before her is unimportant compared with 'the things that happen in your heart', meditates on her condition as she begins the old job of preparing more costumes for yet another play. She ponders the problem of faith vanishing while the need for faith remains:

> . . . given only faith, how can anything else matter? How can anything dismay you if only there is some purpose in the world which you can serve, and which, while serving it, you can understand? Your whole life is illumined by that sense of purpose. . . . in every detail of your life, if no ultimate purpose redeemed it, there was a quality of greyness, of desolation, that could never be described, but which you could feel like a physical pang at your heart. . . . There was, she saw clearly, no possible substitute for faith; no pagan acceptance of life as sufficient to itself, no pantheistic cheer-up stuff, no pseudo-religion of 'progress' with visions of glittering Utopias and ant-heaps of steel and concrete. It is all or nothing. Either life on earth is a preparation for something greater and more lasting, or it is meaningless, dark and dreadful.   CD 315; P 258

She prays for help in her unbelief—and smells the glue almost ready for her to start making another suit of armour:

> The smell of glue was the answer to her prayer. She did not know this. She did not reflect, consciously, that the solution to her difficulty lay in accepting the fact that there was no solution; that if one gets on with the job that lies to hand, the ultimate purpose of the job fades into insignificance; that faith and no faith are very much the same provided that one is doing what is customary, useful and acceptable. CD 318; P 261

The problem vanishes. It begins to get dark and, too busy to light the lamp, she works on.

GORDON COMSTOCK, 'KEEP THE ASPIDISTRA FLYING', 1936

Gordon Comstock—'a pretty bloody name, but then Gordon came of a pretty bloody family'—was born as an unintended child in 1905, the last of a family in that most dismal of classes, the middle-middle, the landless gentry. Its Victorian founder had dynamically plundered both proletariat and foreigner of fifty thousand pounds; its present members are dead-alive, gutless and unsuccessful, drifting along in an atmosphere of semi-genteel failure:

> It was impossible to imagine any of them making any sort of mark in the world, or creating anything, or destroying anything, or being happy, or vividly unhappy, or fully alive, or even earning a decent income. KAF 50; P 43

In the family there are now only deaths, sickness and constant financial harassment:

> It was not *merely* the lack of money. It was rather that, having no money, they still lived mentally in the money-world—the world in which money is virtue and poverty is crime. It was not poverty but the down-dragging of *respectable* poverty that had done for them. They had accepted the money-code, and by that code they were failures. They had never had the sense to lash out and just *live*, money or no money, as the lower classes do. KAF 57; P 49

Year in, year out, nothing ever happens. In Comstock's own branch of the family there are five living members (combined income about £600 per annum; combined ages 263), and they are the kind of people automatically elbowed from the centre of things, never being involved in anything whether it is travel, fighting, imprisonment, marriage or childbirth; and 'there seemed no reason why they should not continue in the same style until they died'.

He grows up in an atmosphere of cut-down clothes and stewed neck of mutton. Huge sums are wasted on him at a third-rate public school where his poverty makes life a continuous conspiracy to keep his end up. Although academically unsuccessful he manages to train his mind along the lines that suit it: reading books denounced by the headmaster; developing unorthodox opinions about the Church of England, patriotism and the Old Boys' Tie; running a school review called *The Bolshevik*. Very early he understands money and the swindle of modern commerce:

> What he realized . . . was that money-worship has been elevated into a religion. Perhaps it is the only real religion—the only really *felt* religion—that is left to us. Money is what God used to be. Good and evil have no meaning any longer except failure and success. Hence the profoundly significant phrase, to *make good*. The decalogue has been reduced to two commandments. One for the employers— the elect, the money-priesthood as it were—'Thou shalt make money'; the other for the employed—the slaves and underlings— 'Thou shalt not lose thy job'.   KAF 56; P 49

The aspidistra symbolizes this money-respectability from which there are only the two escapes of being rich or refusing to be rich. As it is rubbed into Comstock at school that he is a seditious little nuisance who will never be successful, he decides to declare secret war on the money-god, making it his especial purpose *not* to succeed.

Six years at a 'good' job do not destroy his intention of breaking free and writing, for the alternative seems to be the life led by those around him, settling down, making good, selling your soul for a villa and an aspidistra:

> To turn into the typical little bowler-hatted sneak . . . the little docile cit who slips home by the six-fifteen to a supper of cottage

99

pie and stewed tinned pears, half an hour's listening-in to the B.B.C. Symphony Concert, and then perhaps a spot of licit sexual intercourse if his wife 'feels in the mood!' What a fate! No, it isn't like that that one was meant to live. One's got to get right out of it, out of the money-stink.   KAF 61; P 53

His mother's death nerves him to clear out. The consequent months of poverty show him that it is untrue that if you genuinely despise money you can keep going somehow. On the contrary, you are the helpless slave of money until you have enough of it to live on.

A second job is with the New Albion Publicity Company—part of the fungus growing out of modern capitalism, completely modern in spirit, staffed by 'the hard-boiled, Americanized, go-getting type—the type to whom nothing in the world is sacred, except money'. These ad-men have their code: 'the public are swine; advertising is the rattling of a stick inside a swill-bucket'. More than anything else advertising shows a cross-section of the modern world: 'a panorama of ignorance, greed, vulgarity, snobbishness, whoredom, and disease'. One advertisement ('Corner Table Enjoys His Meal With Bovex') gives rise to this meditation:

> Corner Table, heir of the ages; victor of Waterloo, Corner Table. Modern man as his masters want him to be. A docile little porker, sitting in the money-sty, drinking Bovex. . . . Corner Table grins at you, seemingly optimistic, with a flash of false teeth. But what is behind the grin? Desolation, emptiness, prophecies of doom. For can you not see . . . that behind that slick self-satisfaction, that tittering fat-bellied triviality, there is nothing but a frightful emptiness, a secret despair? The great death-wish of the modern world. Suicide pacts. Heads stuck in gas-ovens in lonely maisonettes. French letters and Amen pills. And the reverberations of future wars.
>
> KAF 21; P 19

Comstock's literary gifts make him adept at copy-writing—'the vivid phrase that sticks and rankles, the neat little para. that packs a world of lies into a hundred words'—and he seems to be making good. Before he becomes too involved he has to escape—an action which later seems to him to be the only significant one of his life. Again, working in a book-shop, he has the illusion of being outside the money-world; but what started as an heroic gesture becomes a dingy habit. There is no hardship; but there is constant humiliation. There is the mental deadness and spiritual squalor that inevitably comes when your income reaches a certain level. 'Faith, hope, money—only a saint could have the first two without having the third.' Poverty is spiritual halitosis. Its world is a filthy sub-existence, a spiritual sewer. Cleanness, decency, energy and self-respect all cost money.

Thus, on a November day in the year of blight 1934, Gordon Comstock, a poet whose sole volume fell completely flat two years previously, owns fivepence-halfpenny. His overcoat is up the spout for fifteen shillings; he lives in a house where the hall smells of dishwater, cabbage, rag-mats and bedroom slops, and where you can't go to the W.C. without the feeling that someone is listening to you. He is lonely, moth-eaten, his mind sticky with boredom. He loathes the books which daily surround him because they remind him of his own sterile involvement in a labyrinthine mess of words called *London Pleasures*, a long poem whose conception had been one of the reasons for his choosing poverty, but with which he can now only futilely tinker:

> Could you write even a penny novelette without money to put heart in you? Invention, energy, wit, style, charm—they've all got to be paid for in hard cash. KAF 15; P 14

The city he lives in, whose pleasures he is supposed to be describing, is not a community but merely isolated clusters of meaningless lives drifting drowsily and chaotically to the grave. He and the rest are corpses, rotting upright. Thirty years of futility have led him into a blind alley: you serve the money-god or you go under. Social failure, artistic failure, sexual failure—'And lack of money is at the bottom of them all'.

> He had a vision of London, of the western world; he saw a thousand million slaves toiling and grovelling about the throne of money. The earth is ploughed, ships sail, miners sweat in dripping tunnels underground, clerks hurry for the eight-fifteen with the fear of the boss eating at their vitals. And even in bed with their wives

they tremble and obey. Obey whom? The money-priesthood, the pink-faced masters of the world. The Upper Crust. A welter of sleek young rabbits in thousand guinea motor cars, of golfing stockbrokers and cosmopolitan financiers, of Chancery lawyers and fashionable Nancy boys, of bankers, newspaper peers, novelists of all four sexes, American pugilists, lady aviators, film stars, bishops, titled poets and Chicago gorillas.   KAF 185; P 160

Even such a view of life is merely the result of wishing that a wage of two quid a week was one of five.

Only two people mean anything to him, and his relationship with both is poisoned by the first rule of his war against money: never take charity. One is Ravelston, editor of a Socialist periodical who is trying to escape from his own class to become an honorary member of the proletariat. The other is Rosemary whom he can afford to meet only in the streets, who loves him but will not sleep with him. There is a film of money between them:

> All human relationships must be purchased with money. If you have no money, men won't care for you, women won't love you; won't, that is, care for you or love you the last little bit that matters. And how right they are, after all! For, moneyless, you are un-lovable. Though I speak with the tongues of men and of angels. But then, if I haven't money, I *don't* speak with the tongues of men and of angels.   KAF 21; P 19

For any woman, a man without a large income is somehow dis-honoured, because he has sinned against the aspidistra: the female message to the male is to chuck away his decency and make more money. Every man has a woman round his neck, dragging him down 'to some beastly little semi-detached villa in Putney, with hire-purchase furniture and a portable radio and an aspidistra in the window'.

With Rosemary he goes on a disastrous hike that starts off with the extravagant happiness of falling into absurd enthusiasms over everything they see, moves through a nasty meal at a pretentious hotel and a quarrel over love-making, and ends with his confession that he has only eightpence left and will have to borrow for the rest of the day. The morning's freedom and adventure was the result of having seven and elevenpence in his pocket. 'It had been a brief victory over the money-god; a morning's apostasy, a holiday in the groves of Ashtaroth. But such things never last.'

Another holiday in the groves of Ashtaroth leads to bigger disaster. An unexpected ten pounds ('It was queer how different you felt with all that money in your pocket. Not opulent merely, but reassured, revivified, reborn') is squandered on an expensive meal followed by a shoddy drinking and whoring expedition which results in his arrest: '. . . if you have no money you don't even know how to spend it when you get it.'

One job lost; a search for another apparently futile—there seems nothing before him now except cadging and destitution, nothing behind him except squalid fooleries. All he wants is to be left alone:

> Free from the nagging consciousness of his failure; free to sink . . . down into quiet worlds where money and effort and moral obligation did not exist. . . . No more sponging on Ravelston! No more blackmail to the gods of decency! Down, down, into the mud—down to the streets, the work-house and the jail. It was only there that he could be at peace. KAF 240; P 209

A ten-hour-a-day, thirty-shillings-a-week job in a Lambeth twopenny lending library seems to provide the underground haven he wants where there are no relatives or friends, no hope, fear, ambition, honour or duty. His night of drunkenness seems to have been a turning point:

> It had dragged him downward with strange suddenness. Before, he had fought against the money-code, and yet he had clung to his wretched remnant of decency. But now it was precisely from decency that he wanted to escape. He wanted to go down, deep down, into some world where decency no longer mattered; to cut the strings of his self-respect, to submerge himself—to *sink*. . . . It was all bound up in his mind with the thought of being *under ground*. He liked to think about the lost people, the under ground people, tramps, beggars, criminals, prostitutes. It is a good world that they inhabit, down there in their frowzy kips and spikes. He liked to think that beneath the world of money there is that great

sluttish underworld where failure and success have no meaning; a
sort of kingdom of ghosts where all are equal. That was where he
wished to be, down in the ghost-kingdom, *below* ambition.

KAF 249; P 217

Losing contact with the world of money and culture, living in a
filthy kip, reading nothing but twopenny weeklies, Comstock
begins to let himself go to pieces, turning away not only from
money but from life itself. He seems to have reached the ghost-
kingdom and the mud, and it is here, out of her magnanimity,
that Rosemary, the only link with the upper world that he has
not been able to sever, finally surrenders to him.

The child thus conceived pulls Comstock out of an existence
where both desires and discontents were dwindling. No longer
do the Bovex advertisements make him wish for a few tons of
TNT to send our civilization to the hell where it belongs. He
decides to take up his old job with the New Albion—to end
his war on money and its gods:

> What had he done? Chucked up the sponge! Broken all his oaths!
> His long and lonely war had ended in ignominious defeat. Circum-
> cise ye your foreskins, saith the Lord. He was coming back to the
> fold, repentant. . . . There was a peculiar sensation, an actual
> physical sensation, in his heart, in his limbs, all over him. What
> was it? Shame, misery, despair? Rage at being back in the clutch of
> money? Boredom when he thought of the deadly future? He
> dragged the sensation forth, faced it, examined it. It was relief. . . .
> Now that the thing was done he felt nothing but relief; relief that
> now at last he had finished with dirt, cold, hunger and loneliness
> and could get back to decent, fully human life.   KAF 290; P 252

In a civilization founded on fear and greed the common man
seems to be able to transmute these basic features into something
nobler. The members of the lower middle class which Comstock
is about to join, although living by the money-code, yet manage
to preserve their decency:

> The money-code as they interpreted it was not merely cynical and
> hoggish. They had their standards, their inviolable points of honour.
> They 'kept themselves respectable'—kept the aspidistra flying.
> Besides, they were *alive*. They were bound up in the bundle of life.

They begot children, which is what the saints and the soul-savers never by any chance do. KAF 293; P 255

He drops the manuscript of *London Pleasures*—the work that was to be created outside the money-world—down a drain. At the New Albion he writes the copy ('. . . he did it far better than he had ever done anything else in his life') in a sales campaign for the Queen of Sheba Toilet Requisites Company. He marries, and with Rosemary furnishes a flat. As they return with a newly-bought aspidistra, she feels the baby move inside her: 'Well, once again things were happening in the Comstock family'.

GEORGE BOWLING, 'COMING UP FOR AIR', 1939

Bowling was born in 1893, the younger son of a seed-merchant involved in a race between death and bankruptcy in the Oxfordshire market town of Lower Binfield. Of this world at the end of Victoria's reign he remembers the smells of the shop, of Nailer the dog, of the dustbins; he remembers the noise of the blue-bottles that were everywhere—'And God knows there are worse smells and sounds. Which would you sooner listen to, a blue-bottle or a bombing plane?' At its centre is the vision of his parents, sitting at their fireside reading *The People* or the *News of the World*; or of his mother, cooking 'in a world where she belonged, among things she really understood'. It is a world remembered from forty years on as an eternal summer time, in which 'there were good things to do'.

And of these good things it is fishing which, as something completely opposite to war and modern life, most fully symbolizes the quality of existence before 1914:

> . . . in a manner of speaking I *am* sentimental about my childhood— not my own particular childhood, but the civilization which I grew up in and which is now, I suppose, just about at its last kick. And fishing is somehow typical of that civilization. As soon as you think of fishing you think of things that don't belong to the modern world. The very idea of sitting all day under a willow tree beside a quiet pool—and being able to find a quiet pool to sit beside—belongs to the time before the war, before the radio, before aeroplanes, before Hitler. There's a kind of peacefulness even in the names of

English coarse fish. . . . They're solid kind of names. The people who made them up hadn't heard of machine-guns, they didn't live in terror of the sack or spend their time eating aspirins, going to the pictures, and wondering how to keep out of the concentration camp. . . . Where are the English coarse fish now? When I was a kid every pond and stream had fish in it. Now all the ponds are drained, and when the streams aren't poisoned with chemicals from factories they're full of rusty tins and motor-bike tyres.

CUA 76; P 74

The good things also included reading—mainly the boys' weeklies, particularly *Chums*, and in that paper particularly the serial adventures of Donovan the Dauntless, wandering in exotically remote places. 'A winter day, just warm enough to lie still. . . . I can smell the dust and sainfoin and the cool plastery smell, and I'm up the Amazon, and it's bliss, pure bliss.'

As the years pass, there is work at an eleven-hour day as apprentice grocer; the taking of correspondence courses helping you to get on and set up on your own ('This was before the war, remember, and before the slumps and before the dole. The world was big enough for everyone. Anyone could "set up in trade", there was always room for another shop'). There is the sense of coming trouble with Germany; there is attendance at the vicar's reading-circle; there is making love with the first girl. Nineteen-thirteen, the last year of an era, means the stillness of the water meadows along the Thames, blue hills in the distance, willows up the backwaters, pools as green as grass, the feeling of not being frightened and of not being in a hurry. In many ways life may have been harsher ('You saw ghastly things happening sometimes') yet people had a feeling of security, even when they weren't secure:

More exactly, it was a feeling of continuity. All of them knew they'd got to die, and I suppose a few of them knew they were going to go bankrupt, but what they didn't know was that the order of things could change. Whatever might happen to themselves, things would go on as they'd known them. . . . [his parents] never lived to know that everything they'd believed in was just so much junk. They lived at the end of an epoch, when everything was dissolving into a sort

of ghastly flux, and they didn't know it. They thought it was
eternity. You couldn't blame them. That was what it felt like.

CUA 109; P 107

In the war that destroys this world, Bowling is taken away
from Lower Binfield, wounded, commissioned, and returns
home only once, in 1917, for his mother's funeral. Even then all
is changing: the house where he'd crawled about the kitchen,
where he'd read about Donovan the Dauntless, where he'd mixed
bread paste for his fishing expeditions, was empty. His father's
name has been burned from the shop signboard: 'it had been as
permanent to me as the pyramids, and now it would be just an
accident if I ever set foot in it again'. Nor does he really care.
At the moment he is more concerned with the style of his
officer's trousers, and with the beanos he and the other chaps can
have with the sixty quid his mother has left him.

The effect of the rest of the war, spent—following some
bureaucratic mistake—as officer commanding a non-existent
food dump in Cornwall where there is nothing to do but read,
is to leave Bowling with a disbelief in everything, and a knowledge that everybody else felt the same way, caught in a wave of
disbelief and nihilism:

> People who in a normal way would have gone through life with
> about as much tendency to think for themselves as a suet pudding
> were turned into Bolshies just by the war. What should I be now if
> it hadn't been for the war? I don't know, but something different
> from what I am. If the war didn't happen to kill you it was bound
> to start you thinking. After that unspeakable idiotic mess you
> couldn't go on regarding society as something eternal and un-
> questionable, like a pyramid. You knew it was just a balls-up.

CUA 126; P 123

After this experience he has passed completely out of the orbit
of the old safe existence behind the counter. He wants to be
travelling, 'pulling down the big dough'. Coming to the realities
of post-war life—the chief of which is an everlasting, frantic
struggle to sell things, which in turn involves selling yourself in
order to get a job and keep it—he finally becomes an insurance

107

salesman. Thereafter nothing happens except his marriage to Hilda, daughter of an Anglo-Indian family living in a house designed to preserve for them the illusion of still being in Kipling's India. From the start the marriage is a failure, largely because Hilda quickly settles into the joylessness characteristic of her decayed middle class: 'The essential fact about them is that all their vitality has been drained away by lack of money.'

By 1938 Bowling is the middle-aged middling type, economically average, with the look of a man who sells things on commission: the active, hearty, fat man, 'the athletic bouncing type that's nicknamed Fatty or Tubby and is always the life and soul of the party'. He lives in Ellesmere Road in the inner-outer suburbs of London, where at one house in fifty some anti-social type has painted his front door blue instead of green. The road is a line of prison cells:

> A line of semi-detached torture-chambers where the poor little five-to-ten-pound-a-weekers quake and shiver, every one of them with the boss twisting his tail and the wife riding him like the nightmare and the kids sucking his blood like leeches. There's a lot of rot talked about the sufferings of the working class. I'm not so sorry for the proles myself. Did you ever know a navvy who lay awake thinking about the sack? The prole suffers physically, but he's a free man when he isn't working. But in every one of those little stucco boxes there's some poor bastard who's *never* free except when he's fast asleep and dreaming that he's got the boss down the bottom of a well and is bunging lumps of coal at him.   CUA 14; P 14

Personally he is at the stage where he is tired of fifteen years as husband and father—'. . . the notion of myself as a kind of tame dairy-cow for a lot of women and kids to chase up and down doesn't appeal to me'. The children's conversation is mainly about rulers, pencil boxes and who got top marks in French. His wife is constantly bemoaning petty disasters such as the rising price of butter, the enormous gas bill, the wearing out of the children's shoes, and the imminence of the next instalment on the radio.

This present world is one of fear: 'We swim in it. It's our element. Everyone that isn't scared stiff of losing his job, is scared stiff of war, of Fascism, or Communism, or something.' At an anti-Fascist meeting he attends one evening, Bowling realizes that the speaker is deliberately stirring up hatred against certain foreigners, and that behind the anti-Fascist words there is this kind of vision:

> It's a picture of himself smashing people's faces in with a spanner. Fascist faces, of course. . . . Smash! Right in the middle! The bones cave in like an eggshell and what was a face a minute ago is just a great big blob of strawberry jam. . . . But why? Likeliest explanation, because he's scared. Every thinking person nowadays is stiff with fright. This is merely a chap who's got sufficient foresight to be a little more frightened than the others. Hitler's after us! Quick! Let's all grab a spanner and get together, and perhaps if we smash in enough faces they won't smash ours. CUA 151; P 148

In every shipyard in the world they are riveting up the battle-ships for another war, and there are bombers constantly flying overhead. At the moment London is enormous and peaceful, like a vast wilderness with no wild beasts. But in a few years? Yet the war itself, with its air-raid sirens, its food queues, its 'machine-guns squirting out of bedroom windows', will not be so terrible as the after-war created by the streamlined men from Eastern Europe:

> The world we're going down into, the kind of hate-world, slogan-world. The coloured shirts, the barbed wire, the rubber truncheons. The secret cells where the electric light burns night and day, and the detectives watching you while you sleep. And the processions and the posters with enormous faces, and the crowds of a million people all cheering for the Leader till they deafen themselves into thinking that they really worship him, and all the time, under-neath, they hate him so that they want to puke. CUA 152; P 149

The 1938 world is one as much characterized by the ersatz milk-bar as the 1913 world was characterized by fishing: everything is slick, shiny and streamlined; there is no real food, no comfort, no privacy. It is in one of these places that Bowling eats a frank-furter tasting of fish, and seems to have bitten into the modern world:

> . . . everything made out of something else. Celluloid, rubber, chromium-steel everywhere, arc-lamps blazing all night, glass roofs over your head, radios all playing the same tune, no vegetation left, everything cemented over, mock-turtles grazing under the neutral fruit-trees. But when you come down to brass tacks and get your teeth into something solid, a sausage for instance, that's what you get. Rotten fish in a rubber skin. Bombs of filth bursting inside your mouth. CUA 28; P 27

Somewhere the world has gone wrong. Nearly all the decent people, who don't want to smash faces with spanners, have minds that are stopped. There are only dead men and live gorillas, in a suffocating world where we can never do what we really want to do, where there is time to do everything but the things you feel really worth doing. The good world to live in— the pre-war Lower Binfield—seems gone forever.

Bowling has what he calls a hangover from this past world, and he decides to try to come up for air by returning to his birth-place, alone, at the beginning of the fishing season. Perhaps he can find the peace that once existed in Lower Binfield: 'You can say we were like turnips, if you like. But turnips don't live in terror of the boss, they don't lie awake at night thinking about the next slump and the next war.'

He wants to get his nerve back before the bad times begin on the journey downwards:

> Into the grave, into the cesspool—no knowing. And you can't face that kind of thing unless you've got the right feeling inside you. There's something that's gone out of us in these twenty years since the war. It's a kind of vital juice that we've squirted away until there's nothing left. All this rushing to and fro! Everlasting scramble for a bit of cash. Everlasting din of buses, bombs, radios, telephone bells. Nerves worn all to bits, empty places in our bones where the marrow ought to be. CUA 171; P 168

Even as he goes on his illicit holiday he feels pursued by those who can't understand his need to sneak away, 'and all the mean-minded bastards who *could* understand only too well, and who'd raise heaven and earth to prevent it'.

Inevitably when he does see Lower Binfield again for the first time in twenty years it has been swallowed like one of the lost cities of Peru. The market-town of two thousand has become an industrial development of twenty-five thousand. Bowling is lost in the raw newness of everything: in the market-place the old horse trough has gone; the old pub has been tarted up into a road-house where his name (one of the oldest in the town) is unknown; his home has become Wendy's Tea Shop; the Hall has become a lunatic asylum. On the old tow path ('Often I've sat there a whole afternoon, and a heron might be standing in the shallow water . . . and for three or four hours on end there wouldn't be anyone passing to scare him away') there are bungalows, cars, gramophones. The place is black with people, some of them—ironically—fishing, in a continuous chain (one man every five yards). The river is crammed with boats—'the floats of the poor devils who were trying to fish rocked up and down on the wash of the motor boats'. In any case there are probably no longer any fish in a river whose once luminous green water has become brown, dirty, full of fag-ends and paper bags.

The girl with whom he first made love has become a shambling hag; a conquering army of aliens has filled what was once *his* town with rubbish. And in reality, a secret pool with enormous fish, which he had discovered as a boy but had never been able to try, has been drained and is already half full of tin cans. Trying to visit the scenes of boyhood is useless: 'Coming up for air! But there isn't any air. The dustbin that we're in reaches up to the stratosphere.'

What finally makes Bowling leave the town is the accidental dropping of a bomb by one of the planes that are constantly above it. As he returns to Ellesmere Road, leaving behind him a new and unused fishing rod, he realizes the futility of his attempt to surface; looking for the old life is a waste of time:

> And it was a queer thing I'd done by coming here. All those years Lower Binfield had been tucked away somewhere or other in my mind, a sort of quiet corner that I could step back into when I felt like it, and finally I'd stepped back into it and found that it didn't exist.   CUA 227; P 223

The one thing he has learnt is that it is all going to happen: 'the things you're terrified of, the things that you tell yourself are just a nightmare or only happen in foreign countries.' England, as he drives back across part of it, in its multiplicity and privateness seems enormous, but this will be no protection:

> It doesn't matter how many of them there are, they're all for it. The bad times are coming, and the stream-lined men are coming too. What's coming afterwards I don't know, it hardly even interests me. I only know that if there's anything you care a curse about, better say good-bye to it now, because everything you've ever known is going down, down, into the muck, with the machine-guns rattling all the time. CUA 229; P 225

He returns to the red-brick prison, to a Hilda who will not believe that he hasn't been off with some woman. The whole escapade becomes meaningless in an atmosphere where nothing is real except gas bills, school fees, boiled cabbage and the office on Monday morning. Everything fades out until there is nothing left but a vulgar row in the smell of old mackintoshes.

WINSTON SMITH, 'NINETEEN EIGHTY-FOUR', 1949

Winston Smith was born in the mid-forties. When he was about ten his family disappeared in one of the periodic purges, and he is half-aware that in some way his mother and sister had sacrificed themselves for his sake. The pre-1984 world was one where such a tragic personal sacrifice was still possible (now, it is only the proles—considered to be outside civilization—who maintain such unquestioned private loyalties):

> Tragedy . . . belonged to the ancient time, to a time when there was still privacy, love and friendship, and when the members of a family stood by one another without needing to know the reason. . . . [his mother] had sacrificed herself to a conception of loyalty that was private and unalterable. Such things, he saw, could not happen to-day. To-day there were fear, hatred and pain, but no dignity of emotion, no deep or complex sorrows.

> 1984 33; P 27

An atomic bomb on Colchester, confused street-fighting in London, constant hunger and sordid squabbling to get more than

a fair share of food, the Revolution, life as an orphan in a Re-
clamation Centre, a continuous war against Eastasia or Eurasia,
a hideously unsuccessful marriage which collapsed in the
seventies—these are the experiences through which he has grown
up. By 1984 Smith is thirty-nine: small, frail, suffering from a
varicose ulcer on his leg and from early-morning coughing fits,
living in the collapsing Victory Mansions ('The hallway smelt
of boiled cabbage and old rag mats'). He is a citizen of an England
which has become Airstrip One, a province of a super-state
known as Oceania. He lives in a London on which fall twenty
or thirty rocket bombs a week, where there are rotting houses,
empty bomb-sites, electricity cuts, a chronic shortage of one
thing after another, cold water, gritty soap, cigarettes that fall
to pieces, evil-tasting food, ugly people. And this dinginess, this
barrenness and listlessness seem even more truly characteristic of
modern life than its cruelty and insecurity.

> The ideal set up by the Party was something huge, terrible and
> glittering—a world of steel and concrete, of monstrous machines
> and terrifying weapons—a nation of warriors and fanatics, march-
> ing forward in perfect unity, all thinking the same thoughts and
> shouting the same slogans, perpetually working, fighting, triumph-
> ing, persecuting—three hundred million people all with the same
> face. The reality was decaying, dingy cities where underfed people
> shuffled to and fro in leaky shoes, in patched-up nineteenth-century
> houses that smelt always of cabbage and bad lavatories. He seemed
> to see a vision of London, vast and ruinous, city of a million dust-
> bins. . . .   1984 77; P 62

There are regulation lunches ('a metal pannikin of pinkish-grey
stew, a hunk of bread, a cube of cheese, a mug of milkless Victory
Coffee, and one saccharine tablet'); the Community Centres,
attendance at which is carefully checked; the Junior Anti-Sex
League, designed to destroy the erotic attachment between
people which might set up private loyalties; the Youth League
and the Spies, whose members have been issued with ear-trum-
pets so that they can more easily listen to their parent's conversation. The children have been changed into horrible, ungovern-
able savages, adoring everything connected with the Party:

The songs, the processions, the banners, the hiking, the drilling with dummy rifles, the yelling of slogans, the worship of Big Brother—it was all a sort of glorious game to them. All their ferocity was turned outwards, against the enemies of the State, against foreigners, traitors, saboteurs, thought-criminals. It was almost normal for people over thirty to be frightened of their own children. And with good reason, for hardly a week passed in which the *Times* did not carry a paragraph describing how some eavesdropping little sneak—'child hero' was the phrase generally used—had overheard some compromising remark and denounced its parents to the Thought Police. 1984 28; P 23

The Party apparatus of government is everywhere. Above all it exists in Newspeak (the development of Standard English whose sole aim is the narrowing of the range of thought by the destruction of vocabulary), and in the telescreens of the Thought Police which can receive and transmit simultaneously (a technical advance making possible the destruction of private life). You did not know when you were being watched. Possibly everybody was watched all the time: 'You had to live . . . in the assumption that every sound you made was overheard, and, except in darkness, every movement scrutinized.'

This is the culture of a perverted English Socialism known as Ingsoc, administered from the Ministries of Truth, Peace, Plenty and Love. It is the last that is really frightening: windowless, surrounded by a maze of barbed wire and machine-gun nests. 'Even the streets leading up to its outer barriers were roamed by gorilla-faced guards in black uniforms, armed with jointed truncheons.' Oceania is governed by an élite—the Inner Party (two per cent of the population) which rules on the basis of its slogans: War is Peace, Freedom is Slavery, and Ignorance is Strength. The Party has two major problems: the conquest of the earth, and the prevention of independent thought, science existing only insofar as it helps to achieve these. Its fundamental principle, based on the idea that nothing exists except through human consciousness, is that of reality-control—a lunatic dislocation of the mind that in Newspeak is called 'Doublethink'.

Doublethink means the power of holding two contradictory beliefs in one's mind simultaneously, and accepting both of them. The Party intellectual knows in which direction his memories must be altered; he therefore knows that he is playing tricks with reality; but by the exercise of *doublethink* he also satisfies himself that reality is not violated. The process has to be conscious, or it would not be carried out with sufficient precision, but it also has to be unconscious, or it would bring with it a feeling of falsity and hence of guilt. *Doublethink* lies at the very heart of Ingsoc, since the essential act of the Party is to use conscious deception while retaining the firmness of purpose that goes with complete honesty. To tell deliberate lies while genuinely believing in them, to forget any fact that has become inconvenient, and then, when it becomes necessary again, to draw it back from oblivion for just so long as it is needed, to deny the existence of objective reality and all the while to take account of the reality which one denies—all this is indispensably necessary. Even in using the word *doublethink* it is necessary to exercise *doublethink*. For by using the word one admits that one is tampering with reality; by a fresh act of *doublethink* one erases this knowledge: and so on indefinitely, with the lie always one leap ahead of the truth. Ultimately it is by means of *doublethink* that the Party has been able—and may, for all we know, continue to be able for thousands of years—to arrest the course of history.

1984 220; P 171

History is arrested by continually altering it. In fact there is no past—only a kind of continuous present in which the Party is always right. The slogan is: 'Who controls the present, controls the past.' The doublethinker is the complete Party-man, happy in a world where there are no friends but only comrades, where a love affair is impossible and erotic enjoyment a crime ('for how could the fear, the hatred, and the lunatic credulity which the Party needed in its members be kept at the right pitch, except by bottling down some powerful instinct and using it as a driving force?'). A Party Member has no spare time and is never alone except when in bed. To do anything requiring solitude is dangerous—it suggests that forbidden individualism or eccentricity described by the Newspeak word 'ownlife'.

The greatest evil is 'thoughtcrime'—which will always be discovered—and the greatest virtue is to be 'goodthinkful'.

In Newspeak there is even the concept 'facecrime'—'to wear an improper expression on your face (to look incredulous when a victory was announced, for example)'. There is also the concept of 'crimestop':

> ... the faculty of stopping short, as though by instinct, at the threshold of any dangerous thought. It includes the power of not grasping analogies, of failing to perceive logical errors, of misunderstanding the simplest arguments if they are inimical to Ingsoc, and of being bored or repelled by any train of thought which is capable of leading in a heretical direction. *Crimestop*, in short, means protective stupidity.   1984 217; P 169

The twin poles of this society are Big Brother—infallible, omnipotent, immortal and omnipresent through his gigantic photographs—and Goldstein—Enemy of the People, backslider, anti-revolutionary, defiler of Party purity, author of a terrible book, a compendium of all the heresies, called *The Theory and Practice of Oligarchical Collectivism*.

Smith himself is an Outer Party Member, working a sixty-hour week in the Ministry of Truth at the 'rectification' of records and all documents of any conceivable ideological significance, in order to make them consistent with the changing Party line:

> Day by day and almost minute by minute the past was brought up to date. In this way every prediction made by the Party could be shown by documentary evidence to have been correct; nor was any item of news, or any expression of opinion, which conflicted with the needs of the moment, ever allowed to remain on record. All history was a palimpsest, scraped clean and re-inscribed exactly as often as was necessary. In no case would it have been possible, once the deed was done, to prove that any falsification had taken place.
> 1984 43; P 35

In such a world—compared with a single equation containing two unknowns—he is lost, locked in his loneliness:

> He felt as though he were wandering in the forests of the sea bottom, lost in a monstrous world where he himself was the monster. He was alone. The past was dead, the future was un-

imaginable. What certainty had he that a single human creature now living was on his side? And what way of knowing that the dominion of the Party would not endure *for ever*? . . . Always the eyes watching you and the voice enveloping you. Asleep or awake, working or eating, indoors or out of doors, in the bath or in bed— no escape. Nothing was your own except the few cubic centimetres inside your skull.   1984 30; P 25

And in the end there is not going to be even that final refuge. Perhaps not to accept the Party's claims, not to believe its statistics, was to be ill or insane. Smith looks at a school history book and its frontispiece—the usual, hypnotic, full-face picture of Big Brother:

> It was as though some huge force were pressing down upon you— something that penetrated inside your skull, battering against your brain, frightening you out of your beliefs, persuading you, almost, to deny the evidence of your senses. In the end the Party would announce that two and two made five, and you would have to believe it. It was inevitable that they should make that claim sooner or later: the logic of their position demanded it. Not merely the validity of experience, but the very existence of external reality, was tacitly denied by their philosophy. The heresy of heresies was common sense. And what was terrifying was not that they would kill you for thinking otherwise, but that they might be right.
>
>   1984 84; P 67

But sanity, he heretically thinks, is not statistical. The correctness of an opinion is not proportionate to the number of people holding it. You cannot make two and two into whatever is convenient, or reject the evidence of your senses merely because the Party orders you to. However enormous 'their' power, however brilliant 'their' reasoning, 'they' were wrong. Truisms are true, and salvation lay in holding on to that fact. 'Freedom is the freedom to say that two plus two make four. If that is granted, all else follows.' That is one of the first entries in the diary he begins to keep, writing in a corner of his room that by an accident of construction is out of range of the telescreen.

This rebellious attempt to carry on the human heritage ('a lonely ghost uttering a truth that nobody would ever hear') has other manifestations. During the Hates he comes to feel a sympathy with Goldstein: '. . . his heart went out to the lonely, derided heretic on the screen, sole guardian of truth and sanity in a world of lies'. He hopes that the proles (not indoctrinated with Party ideology, and given intellectual freedom because they have no intellects) will eventually rebel and take over the future. He comes to believe in the existence of an anti-revolutionary organization known as the Brotherhood, rumoured to be led by Goldstein. He refuses to control his memory, and in his pursuit of 'ownlife' even toys with the idea of renting a room he has discovered above a second-hand shop in one of the prole districts —a room apparently without a telescreen. Although the idea has to be rejected as impossible, the sight of the room has awakened a nostalgic, ancestral memory. He seems to know what it is like to sit in such a room, 'utterly alone, utterly secure, with nobody watching you, no voice pursuing you, no sound except the singing of the kettle and the friendly ticking of the clock'.

Above all there is his relationship with Julia and O'Brien. Julia works in the fiction department of the Ministry of Truth, servicing a motor that operates a fiction-writing machine. Her reputation for purity is such that she has even been allowed to work in the Muck House—Pornosec, which produces pornography for the consumption of the proles. Believing that safety lies in always yelling with the crowd, she has built up a façade of loyalty, attending demonstrations, distributing literature for the Junior Anti-Sex League, preparing banners for Hate Week. It all paid: 'If you kept the small rules, you could break the big ones'. But such rule-breaking is caused purely by her desire for erotic pleasure; however well-versed she is in the tactics of deception it is not because of any rational or ideological repulsion from Ingsoc. She is a rebel only from the waist down:

> Life as she saw it was quite simple. You wanted a good time; 'they', meaning the Party, wanted to stop you having it; you broke the rules as best you could. She seemed to think it just as natural that 'they' should want to rob you of your pleasures as that you should want to avoid being caught. She hated the Party, and said so in the crudest words, but she made no general criticism of it.
>
> 1984 135; P 108

118

Because she has recognized him as one who does not belong, she sends Smith the most heretical message possible in Oceania: 'I love you.' After days of frustration and snatched moments of muttered instructions, they begin their sexual relationship out of the range of telescreens and microphones in a countryside that reminds him of a boyhood dream-landscape which he has called the Golden Country. But from the beginning this relationship is associated with corruption. When he learns that she has done this before with scores of Outer Party members he is delighted. Perhaps the Party is rotten under its surface cult of strenuousness and self-denial. 'If he could have infected the whole lot of them with leprosy or syphilis, how gladly he would have done so! Anything to rot, to weaken, to undermine!' Just making love, satisfying mere lust, is impossible in a world where everything has become political, and where everything is mixed with fear and hate: 'Their embrace had been a battle, the climax a victory. It was blow struck against the Party.'

For Smith the whole experience is involved in a defeat Julia refuses to think about—just as she refuses to interest herself in his anxieties about the destruction of history:

> She would not accept it as a law of nature that the individual is always defeated. In a way she realized that she herself was doomed, that sooner or later the Thought Police would catch her and kill her, but with another part of her mind she believed that it was somehow possible to construct a secret world in which you could live as you chose. All you needed was luck and cunning and boldness. She did not understand that there was no such thing as happiness, that the only victory lay in the far future, long after you were dead, that from the moment of declaring war on the Party it was better to think of yourself as a corpse.   1984 139; P 111

There are only isolated times when any prolonged intimacy is possible. Most of their relationship has to be developed in public; their conversation is like that of experienced convicts at exercise, flicking on and off as they leave or approach any manifestation of the Party's authority.

Any love affair is predestined to end in the cells of the Ministry of Love. But in the room over the second-hand shop (which he does finally rent) Smith almost establishes contact with an ancient world where such a private life was possible as an accepted thing: a cool summer evening, making love when you choose, talking about what you choose, 'simply lying there and listening to peaceful sounds outside. Surely there could never have been a time when that seemed ordinary?'.

As his physical condition improves ('The process of life had ceased to be intolerable, he had no longer any impulse to make faces at the telescreen or shout curses at the top of his voice'), even he tries to persuade himself that 'they' can be beaten. Even he comes to think that the fundamental aspect of 'ownlife'— the integrity of the real feeling of the inner heart as opposed to whatever the brain may be made to confess after torture—could not be destroyed. 'They' cannot get inside you:

> He thought of the telescreen with its never-sleeping ear. They could spy upon you night and day, but if you kept your head you could still outwit them. With all their cleverness they had never mastered the secret of finding out what another human being was thinking. Perhaps that was less true when you were actually in their hands. . . . Facts, at any rate, could not be kept hidden. They could be tracked down by enquiry, they could be squeezed out of you by torture. But if the object was not to stay alive but to stay human, what difference did it ultimately make? They could not alter your feelings: for that matter you could not alter them yourself, even if you wanted to. They could lay bare in the utmost detail everything that you had done or said or thought; but the inner heart, whose workings were mysterious even to yourself, remained impregnable.
>
> 1984 171; P 136

O'Brien is an Inner Party member with whom Smith believes he has shared a moment of telepathic rebellion during one of the two-minute Hates: 'There was a link of understanding between them, more important than affection or partisanship.' He comes to think that O'Brien, something in whose face suggests political unorthodoxy, is a leader of The Brotherhood. He feels an impulse 'simply to walk into O'Brien's presence, announce that he was the enemy of the Party, and demand his help'. He realizes that it is for O'Brien that he is keeping the diary.

As in the first relationship with Julia, here also the first move comes from the other side. Smith is invited to call at O'Brien's flat on the pretence of borrowing a new edition of the Newspeak dictionary. Smith feels that at last he has reached the outer edge of the conspiracy—and again the move is associated with death, with stepping into the dampness of a grave he has always known to be there waiting for him.

O'Brien claims that Goldstein and the Brotherhood really exist as anti-Party forces, and for their sake both Smith and Julia swear to do anything to weaken or demoralize the Party—except to separate and not see each other again. As in the sexual love which leads them to make this exception, so in work for the Brotherhood the end will be personal defeat. O'Brien tells them that they are joining the dead: 'there is no possibility that any perceptible changes will happen within our own lifetime. . . . our only true life is in the future.'

Both these relationships find their ending when Smith is arrested and confronted by the Thought Police in the windowless but constantly lighted Ministry of Love.

Here there is no sense of time or place. In the unending procession of criminals there is constant squalor and terror, and frequent horrified reference to a mysterious Room 101. Smith undergoes the usual preliminary beatings-up with five or six men at him simultaneously with fists, truncheons, steel rods or boots:

> There were times when he rolled about the floor, as shameless as an animal, writhing his body this way and that in an endless, hopeless effort to dodge the kicks, and simply inviting more and yet more kicks, in his ribs, in his belly, on his elbows, on his shins, in his groin, in his testicles, on the bone at the base of his spine. There were times when it went on and on until the cruel, wicked, unforgivable thing seemed to him not that the guards continued to beat him but that he could not force himself into losing consciousness. 1984 246; P 193

The Guardian of the Human Spirit finally becomes a snivelling bundle of bones in dirty underclothes, hair and teeth falling out, stinking like a goat, looking like a sixty-year-old man suffering from a malignant disease, a graceless bag of filth. By the Party interrogators who work on him in relays he is reduced to psychological pulp:

> Their real weapon was the merciless questioning that went on and on, hour after hour, tripping him up, laying traps for him, twisting everything that he said, convicting him at every step of lies and self-contradiction, until he began weeping as much from shame as from nervous fatigue. . . . Most of the time they screamed abuse at him and threatened at every hesitation to deliver him over to the guards again; but sometimes they would suddenly change their tune, call him comrade, appeal to him in the name of Ingsoc and Big Brother, and ask him sorrowfully whether even now he had not enough loyalty to the Party left to make him wish to undo the evil he had done.
>
> 1984 247; P 194

Directing the operation is O'Brien: tormentor, protector, inquisitor and friend—the teacher taking pains with a wayward but promising child, the mentor who will save Smith from his mental derangement and defective memory, the mind-moulder who will re-integrate the heretic, and lead the lunatic back to sanity. Men are infinitely malleable. In the Ministry of Love they are not punished but cured—taught to make the effort of will necessary to liberate themselves from their diseased attempt to live 'ownlife'. O'Brien lectures Smith on humility:

> 'You would not make the act of submission which is the price of sanity. You preferred to be a lunatic, a minority of one. Only the disciplined mind can see reality, Winston. You believe that reality is something objective, external, existing in its own right. You also believe that the nature of reality is self-evident. When you delude yourself into thinking that you see something, you assume that everyone else sees the same thing as you. But I tell you, Winston, that reality is not external. Reality exists in the human mind, and nowhere else. Not in the individual mind, which can make mistakes, and in any case soon perishes: only in the mind of the Party, which is collective and immortal. Whatever the Party holds to be truth, *is* truth. It is impossible to see reality except by looking through the eyes of the Party.'
>
> 1984 254; P 200

He tells of the completeness and perfection of the coming surrender when the flaw in the pattern will be corrected, by the flaw himself:

> 'We do not destroy the heretic because he resists us: so long as he resists us we never destroy him. We convert him, we capture his inner mind, we reshape him. We burn all evil and all illusion out of him; we bring him over to our side, not in appearance, but genuinely, heart and soul. We make him one of ourselves before we kill him. It is intolerable to us that an erroneous thought should exist anywhere in the world, however secret and powerless it may be. Even in the instant of death we cannot permit any deviation. In the old days the heretic walked to the stake still a heretic, proclaiming his heresy, exulting in it. . . . But we make the brain perfect before we blow it out. The command of the old despotisms was 'Thou shalt not'. The command of the totalitarians was 'Thou shalt'. Our command is '*Thou art*'. . . . What happens to you here is for ever. Understand that in advance. We shall crush you down to the point from which there is no coming back. . . . Never again will you be capable of ordinary human feeling. Everything will be dead inside you. Never again will you be capable of love, or friendship, or joy of living, or laughter, or curiosity, or courage, or integrity. You will be hollow. We shall squeeze you empty, and then we shall fill you with ourselves.' 1984 261; P 204

To be free is to be powerless and to be defeated. The Party slogan says: Freedom is Slavery.

It is for the sake of power that the Party exists. Unlike previous totalitarian régimes, it does not pretend to have taken over power in order to create a Utopia. Power is an end in itself: 'One does not establish a dictatorship in order to safeguard a revolution; one makes the revolution in order to establish the dictatorship'. And the power can best be asserted by inflicting suffering on others. O'Brien says:

> 'Power is in inflicting pain and humiliation. Power is in tearing human minds to pieces and putting them together again in new shapes of your own choosing. Do you begin to see, then, what kind of world we are creating? It is the exact opposite of the stupid hedonistic Utopias that the old reformers imagined. A world of

fear and treachery and torment, a world of trampling and being trampled on, a world which will grow not less but *more* merciless as it refines itself. Progress in our world will be progress towards more pain. . . . In our world there will be no emotions except fear, rage, triumph, and self-abasement. Everything else we shall destroy —everything. Already we are breaking down the habits of thought which have survived from before the Revolution. We have cut the links between child and parent, and between man and man, and between man and woman. No one dares trust a wife or a child or a friend any longer. . . . There will be no loyalty, except loyalty towards the Party. There will be no love, except the love of Big Brother. There will be no laughter except the laugh of triumph over a defeated enemy. There will be no art, no literature, no science. . . . But always—do not forget this, Winston—always there will be the intoxication of power, constantly increasing and constantly growing subtler. Always, at every moment, there will be the thrill of victory, the sensation of trampling on an enemy who is helpless. If you want a picture of the future, imagine a boot stamping on a human face—for ever.'   1984 272; P 214

Through his hard struggle to learn, understand and accept that two and two make whatever the Party chooses, Smith's relationship with O'Brien becomes deeper until it perversely reaches the ideal one that should exist between the teacher and the taught:

O'Brien was a person who could be talked to. Perhaps one did not want to be loved so much as to be understood. . . . In some sense that went deeper than friendship, they were intimates. . . .

1984 258; P 202

Smith makes progress in his lessons. He can almost understand that two and two do make five; that, as the immortal collective brain of mankind, the Party must always be right; that sanity is statistical. He exercises himself in 'crimestop'. But once he reverts to his dream of the Golden Country, and wakes crying out for Julia. He has surrendered only in his mind; his heart is still treacherously given to private things. He knew that he was in the wrong, but preferred to be so. He contemplates the final rebellious gesture of hatred for Big Brother that his integrity can make. If there can be no 'ownlife' in living, it can at least be claimed at the moment of dying; in the few seconds when you know they are going to shoot, you can turn the world inside you over, and drop the camouflage:

> . . . bang! would go the batteries of his hatred. Hatred would fill him like an enormous roaring flame. And almost in the same instant bang! would go the bullet, too late, or too early. They would have blown his brain to pieces before they could reclaim it. The heretical thought would be unpunished, unrepented, out of their reach for ever. They would have blown a hole in their own perfection. To die hating them, that was freedom. 1984 287; P 226

The final cure for this relapse ('You must love Big Brother. It is not enough to obey him: you must love him') is provided in Room 101 where there waits for everyone what he most fears in the world—in Smith's case, rats. With these creatures inches from his nose, he betrays his heart: he really wants them to eat into Julia's face rather than into his own.

Cured, he returns to the outside world, even to a job better paid than the one he had before. He is anxious about impending news from the battlefront. He has met Julia but they are completely meaningless to one another. When the news does come over the telescreen it is of a tremendous victory. In his joy at the Party's triumph, Smith looks again at the nearby picture of Big Brother:

> He gazed up at the enormous face. Forty years it had taken him to learn what kind of smile was hidden beneath the dark moustache. O cruel, needless misunderstanding! O stubborn, self-willed exile from the loving breast! Two gin-scented tears trickled down the sides of his nose. But it was all right, everything was all right, the struggle was finished. He had won the victory over himself. He loved Big Brother. 1984 304; P 239

CONCENTRATION CAMP LITERATURE

Christmas parties in the quaint old house with a sweetly, womanly wife, everything safe, soft, peaceful and domestic— this is not the only facet of the Dickens world, although it may be the one that comes first to mind. When Dickens was ten, his father was arrested and imprisoned for debt, and he himself was put to work sticking labels on tins of blacking. David

Copperfield, similarly employed, describes the experience in words almost identical with those of Dickens's autobiographical account:

> No words can express the secret agony of my soul as I sunk into this companionship; compared these henceforth every-day associates with those of my happier childhood . . .; and felt my hopes of growing up to be a learned and distinguished man crushed in my bosom. The deep remembrance of the sense I had of being utterly without hope now; of the shame I felt in my position; of the misery it was to my young heart to believe that day by day what I had learned, and thought, and delighted in, and raised my fancy and my emulation up by, would pass away from me, little by little, never to be brought back any more; cannot be written.   (CHAP. 11)

(Orwell quotes part of the passage in his essay on Dickens.)

Perhaps it is not entirely fanciful to see in the Blacking Factory and its degradation of the individuals who worked there a prototype of the concentration camp, or at least of the kinds of society in which Orwell's heroes find themselves: Flory in the sahibs' Burma of the early 1920's; Dorothy Hare in the Kent hopfields, or Trafalgar Square, or The Ringwood Academy for Girls of the early thirties; Comstock in the money-rotten London of the middle thirties; Bowling in the prison-cell suburbs, streamlined snackbars and dustbin community of the late thirties; Smith in a society which has its pivot in the cells of the Ministry of Love in the 1980's.

For most of these characters (Dorothy Hare is the one who fits least easily into this pattern) such a life is suffocating in its sense of dislocation, its sense that somewhere, somehow, human existence has taken a wrong turning. Flory has his dream of a return to the free air of England, or, failing that, of living in Burma with a sympathetic soul-mate; Comstock has his dream of a life outside greed and money-grubbing; Bowling has a dream of a summer world revolving round fishing which had existed before the First World War; Smith has a dream of the kind of private life accepted as normal before the coming of Ingsoc. In the light of these visions these men try to re-direct their lives against the current set up by the lives of those who surround them and who make up their respective communities.

David Copperfield runs away from Murdstone and Grinby's bottling warehouse in Chapter 12 to join Betsey Trotwood and Mr. Dick, and to make, in Chapter 15, 'another beginning'. Almost fifty chapters and five hundred pages later he looks over the story he has told, and comments on his present state:

> I see myself, with Agnes at my side, journeying along the road of life. I see our children and our friends around us; and I hear the roar of many voices, not indifferent to me as I travel on.

Aunt Betsey, Mr. Dick, Peggotty, the Doctor and his Dictionary, Traddles and Sophy are there—but above all Agnes, his second wife:

> But, one face, shining on me like a Heavenly light by which I see all other objects, is above them and beyond them all. And that remains. I turn my head, and see it, in its beautiful serenity, beside me. . . . Oh Agnes, Oh my soul, so may thy face be by me when I close my life indeed; so may I, when realities are melting from me like the shadows which I now dismiss, still find thee near me, pointing upward! (CHAP. 64)

Not much to our taste, perhaps; certainly very different from the last pages of the novels described in this chapter: Dorothy Hare physically repelled by Warburton, the only man to befriend her; Elizabeth turning from a Flory she regards as a moral leper; Hilda Bowling quarrelling with her husband over a suspected infidelity; Julia betraying a lover who will soon betray her— only with Rosemary and Gordon Comstock is the pattern lost.

Orwell made occasional reference to what he called 'concentration camp literature', lacking in England because English writers could not see themselves as victims. Orwell could so see himself, and his fiction is a contribution to the genre he named.

6

The Free Intelligence

Any professional writer must recognize the importance of the written word which is his bread and butter. The more serious he is, the more will he be conscious of this; the more intensely will he struggle to develop his skill in the manipulation of language, to use it as accurately as possible ('accurately' meaning not necessarily 'in accordance with the rules of school grammar' but certainly meaning 'in accordance with what he really wants to say'). Also the more concerned will he be with the general state of language as it is being used in his society. Because written language is fundamental to civilization—it allows communication between members at a great distance; it allows cultural records to be kept and thus passed on to future generations; it allows problems to be solved by other than violent means—its function is a political and social question as well as a linguistic and literary one.

Thus, when Orwell wrote a book called *The English People* he included a chapter on the English language. When he wrote *Nineteen Eighty-Four* he went to the length of describing, both in the novel itself and in an appendix, the nature of the new language that the society of Oceania was developing. In his concern for language, especially as it was used in totalitarian states, Orwell brought together the literary and political halves of his career. His ideas on the subject provide a useful summary of his central interest—the working of what he called 'the free intelligence'.

One of the best-known statements of the importance of a

healthy language was made (ironically, in this context, because Orwell often referred to him as a Fascist) by Ezra Pound in an essay called 'How to Read' (reprinted in *Literary Essays of Ezra Pound*, ed. T. S. Eliot):

> Save in the rare and limited instances of invention in the plastic arts, or in mathematics, the individual cannot think and communicate his thought, the governor and legislator cannot act effectively or frame his laws, without words, and the solidity and validity of these words is in the care of the damned and despised *litterati*. When their work goes rotten—by that I do not mean when they express indecorous thoughts—but when their very medium, the very essence of their work, the application of word to thing goes rotten, i.e. becomes slushy and inexact, or excessive or bloated, the whole machinery of social and of individual thought and order goes to pot. This is a lesson of history, and a lesson not yet half learned. 21

Orwell makes very much the same point in 'Politics and the English Language' (1946):

> Now, it is clear that the decline of a language must ultimately have political and economic causes: it is not due simply to the bad influence of this or that individual writer. But an effect can become a cause, reinforcing the original cause and producing the same effect in an intensified form, and so on indefinitely. . . . [The English language] becomes ugly and inaccurate because our thoughts are foolish, but the slovenliness of our language makes it easier for us to have foolish thoughts. SE 84; COL E 337

Usually Orwell's starting point was the social order gone to pot, where all issues were public and political rather than personal and private, and where politics itself had become 'a mass of lies, evasions, folly, hatred and schizophrenia'. Thus he surmised that, in the generally bad atmosphere of totalitarianism, languages such as Italian, German and Russian would have deteriorated during recent decades 'as a result of dictatorship'.

For him the solution to the problem of the slush, inexactitude and bloatedness that Pound thought symptomatic of social decay was in simplicity, in letting the meaning choose the word and not the other way about. The writer must hold on to *things*, and not surrender to verbiage. His essay on Yeats—another 'Fascist'—begins by suggesting a connection between a 'wayward, even tortured style' and a 'rather sinister view of life'. And in the essay already quoted he suggests, again with reference to the connection between the present political chaos and the decay of language, that some improvement can be made by starting at the verbal end:

> If you simplify your English, you are freed from the worst follies of orthodoxy. You cannot speak any of the necessary dialects [i.e. jargons and clichés], and when you make a stupid remark its stupidity will be obvious, even to yourself. Political language . . . is designed to make lies sound truthful and murder respectable, and to give an appearance of solidity to pure wind. One cannot change this all in a moment, but one can at least change one's own habits. . . .
>
> SE 101; COL E 351

Modern political writers used language as if it were a Meccano set or a collection of long strips of words, already set in order by someone else and merely needing to be gummed together— a process which was 'the unavoidable result of self-censorship'. Simple, plain, vigorous language, on the other hand, was possible only as a result of fearless thought; it was a symptom of 'ownlife' and consequently of political unorthodoxy:

> In our time it is broadly true that political writing is bad writing. Where it is not true, it will generally be found that the writer is some kind of rebel, expressing his private opinions and not a 'party line'. Orthodoxy, of whatever colour, seems to demand a lifeless, imitative style.
>
> SE 95; COL E 346

Discussing the third book of *Gulliver's Travels*, Orwell noted Swift's perception that one of the aims of totalitarianism was not merely to ensure that people would think the right thoughts, but also actually to make them less conscious. Thus in the Oceania of *Nineteen Eighty-Four* the official language is Newspeak — 'a medium of expression for the world-view and mental habits proper to the devotees of Ingsoc', and also a medium making any other, heretical mode of thought inexpressible. This is a kind of anti-language whose vocabulary will diminish year after year, because the ultimate point of orthodoxy is unconsciousness.

> Its vocabulary was so constructed as to give exact and often very
> subtle expression to every meaning that a Party member could
> properly wish to express, while excluding all other meanings and
> also the possibility of arriving at them by indirect methods. This
> was done partly by the invention of new words, but chiefly by
> eliminating undesirable words and by stripping such words as
> remained of unorthodox meanings, and so far as possible of all
> secondary meanings whatever. . . . Newspeak was designed not
> to extend but to *diminish* the range of thought, and this purpose was
> indirectly assisted by cutting the choice of words down to a mini-
> mum.   1984 305; P 241

POLITICS AND THE WRITER

The members of Pound's damned and despised *literati* to whom
the validity of language is entrusted were therefore central
figures in a political age experiencing the challenge of both right-
and left-wing totalitarianism. In the past they had been the pre-
eminent exponents of 'ownlife'. They were the representatives
of the old culture of post-Renaissance, West European Protestant-
ism—of the Liberal Christianity which seemed, in the years
after 1914, to be at its last gasp. From now on, Orwell wrote in
'Inside the Whale' (1940), the all-important fact for a creative
writer to understand was that the autonomous individual was
going to be stamped out, and it was not a writer's world. His
attitude might have to be passive, quietist—accepting, enduring
and recording developments he could not pretend to control.
Literature as we knew it was coming to an end. The traditional
writer was sitting on a melting iceberg—'merely an anachronism,
a hangover from the bourgeois age, as surely doomed as the
hippopotamus'.

In the modern state all channels of production were coming
under the control of bureaucratic monopolists out to destroy
(or at least to castrate) the artist. Writers were becoming minor
officials, never able to tell what seemed to them the whole of the
truth, directed to work on themes handed down by authority.
Even to the intellectuals themselves, daring to stand alone had

come to seem ideologically criminal. In an essay called 'The Prevention of Literature' (1946) Orwell wrote:

> Poetry *might* survive in a totalitarian age, and certain arts or half-arts, such as architecture, might even find tyranny beneficial, but the prose writer would have no choice between silence and death. Prose literature as we know it is the product of rationalism, of the Protestant centuries, of the autonomous individual. And the destruction of intellectual liberty cripples the journalist, the socio-logical writer, the historian, the novelist, the critic, and the poet, in that order.   SE 128; COL E 320

If the literature of liberalism was at an end, the literature of totalitarianism had not yet appeared—indeed Orwell found it 'barely imaginable'. Yet hints of what it might be like can be seen from the type of work produced in Soviet Russia according to the theory of what is known as 'Socialist Realism'. In view of Orwell's hostile attitude to Stalinism it is worth pursuing this point for some distance.

In 1932 a statute of the Union of Soviet Writers called for

> ... the creation of works of high artistic significance, saturated with the heroic struggle of the international proletariat, with the grandeur of the victory of socialism, and reflecting the great wisdom and heroism of the Communist Party.

In 1959 a Party Central Committee Address to the Third Congress of Soviet Writers asked them

> ... to show truthfully and vividly the beauty of the people's labour exploits ... to be passionate propagandists of the Seven Year Plan, and to imbue the hearts of the Soviet people with courage and energy.

This concept of literature as an ideological weapon on the 'culture front' could lead to developments such as the following.

A Soviet novelist called Fadeyev, Secretary General of the Writers' Union, wrote a novel entitled *The Young Guard* which dealt with the resistance to the Germans offered by the Communist Youth Groups. In 1946 the book was awarded a Stalin Prize. In December of the following year Fadeyev was told that his novel had been wrong to describe Soviet disorganization in the face of the advancing Germans; it had also been wrong in omitting 'the main thing which characterizes the life, growth and work of a Komsomol [i.e. a member of a youth group]— the guiding, educational role of the Party and the Party organization'. Fadeyev revised his novel, a new version of which appeared in 1951.

In 1958 there was the controversy over the publication abroad of Pasternak's novel *Doctor Zhivago*, and the award of a Nobel Prize to its author. On October 26th of that year *Pravda* published an article entitled 'Reactionary Propaganda Uproar over a Literary Weed'. This is part of it:

> . . . the best and leading portion of the Russian intelligentsia . . . greeted the Socialist Revolution with tremendous sympathy and devoted its forces to honest service to the people. The historic struggle for the new order, against the forces of bourgeois reaction that had banded together, the heroic deeds of the Soviet people which engaged in single combat against the world of oppression, blood and filth, carried along and inspired poets, writers and artists. . . . Pasternak tried to join this movement, to readjust himself, to become at least a fellow-traveller. . . . But Pasternak did not go any further. Hostility towards Marxism in philosophy, hostility towards realism in literature, were too deep-rooted in the soul of this intellectual who was bourgeois through and through. Our country marched from victory to victory, a new culture grew and took shape on the basis of socialist construction, new people were being educated; everything was changing around Pasternak, but he remained unchanged. He lagged more and more behind life which was marching forward. . . . He could not find the words needed to become a truly Soviet writer, for whom it is a sacred duty and foremost obligation to serve the people. All this was empty verbiage for the self-enamoured Narcissus. . . . It is obvious that a long stay in the dark corner of his individualism had destroyed in Pasternak any sense of belonging to the Soviet people, destroyed in him the feeling, so habitual to us, of the dignity of the Soviet citizen and patriot. He arranged for himself, of his own accord, the semblance of an émigré existence. He broke off living ties with the Soviet writers' collective. . . . [*Doctor Zhivago*] is a malicious lampoon on the Socialist Revolution, on the Soviet people, on the Soviet

133

intelligentsia. The embittered philistine gave vent to his revengeful gall. He tried to blacken everything new that was ushered in by the Revolution, to justify and extol everything old and counter-revolutionary. . . . By all his activity Pasternak confirms that in our socialist country, gripped by enthusiasm for the building of the radiant Communist society, he is a weed.

(The whole article is reprinted in Robert Conquest's *Courage of Genius*, Collins, 1961.) In fairness, it should be pointed out that much more recognizably Western attitudes to literature have been published in the Soviet Union. A more temperate rejection of Pasternak's novel can be found in the letter sent to him by the editors of the magazine *Novy Mir*, explaining why they could not serialize the work. (This text is reprinted in Edward Crankshaw's book *Khrushchev's Russia*, Penguin, 1959.)

This particular problem was made difficult for Orwell since he was as convinced as the Soviet literary theoreticians that an 'émigré writer', who tried to contract out of his own society, was damaged because he was cutting himself off from the working life of a community. Both Orwell and the Russian critics share a belief in the necessity of what we now call 'committed literature'. For Orwell there was no point in arguing that a liberal dis-interestedness could be preserved only by keeping out of politics, for this was exactly what the 20th-century intellectual could not do. He once wrote: '. . . the opinion that art should have nothing to do with politics is itself a political attitude'. In 'Writers and Leviathan' (1948) he stated:

This is a political age. War, Fascism, concentration camps, rubber truncheons, atomic bombs, etc., are what we daily think about, and therefore to a great extent what we write about, even when we do not name them openly. We cannot help this. When you are on a sinking ship, your thoughts will be about sinking ships. But not only is our subject matter narrowed, but our whole attitude towards literature is coloured by loyalties which we at least inter-mittently realize to be non-literary. . . . the invasion of literature by politics was bound to happen. It must have happened, even if the special problem of totalitarianism had never arisen, because we have developed a sort of compunction which our grandparents did not have, an awareness of the enormous injustice and misery of the world, and a guilt-stricken feeling that one ought to be doing something about it, which makes a purely aesthetic attitude towards life impossible. No one, now, could devote himself to literature as single-mindedly as Joyce or Henry James. But unfortunately, to accept political responsibility now means yielding oneself over to orthodoxies and 'party lines', with all the timidity and dishonesty that that implies. As against the Victorian writers, we have the disadvantage of living among clear-cut political ideologies and of usually knowing at a glance what thoughts are heretical.

EYE 17; COL E 427

Thus the novelist, although not compelled to write directly about contemporary history, was generally either a footler or an idiot if he disregarded the major public events of his time. The novelist, more than most writers, had a 'message' which would influence even the smallest details of his work. All art was propaganda (although not all propaganda was art). In his discussion of Henry Miller, whom he met on the way to Spain ('What most intrigued me about him was to find that he felt no interest in the Spanish war whatever'), Orwell suggests how difficult it is to see literary merit in a book attacking your own deepest beliefs.

This meant that your judgment of a work of art could not be divorced from your criteria as a member of a human society. For example, you had to be able to say—of a picture by Salvador Dali—that it was wonderfully drawn and that it was evil. You could not regard it as morally neutral, as a coloured design, any more than you could regard literature merely as the manipulation of words. In 'Benefit of Clergy' (1944), Orwell reviewed Dali's autobiography and some of his painting, all of which he saw as an assault on sanity and decency:

> . . . in his outlook, his character, the bedrock decency of a human being does not exist. He is as anti-social as a flea. Clearly such people are undesirable, and a society in which they can flourish has something wrong with it. . . . One ought to be able to hold in one's head simultaneously the two facts that Dali is a good draughtsman and a disgusting human being. The one does not invalidate or, in a sense,

affect the other. The first thing that we demand of a wall is that it shall stand up. If it stands up, it is a good wall, and the question of what purpose it serves is separable from that. And yet even the best wall in the world deserves to be pulled down if it surrounds a concentration camp. In the same way it should be possible to say, 'This is a good book or a good picture, and it ought to be burned by the public hangman'. Unless one can say that, at least in imagination, one is shrinking [sic] the implications of the fact that an artist is also a citizen and a human being.　　　CE 141; COL E 213

Pasternak (say the Russians) is a weed; Dali (says Orwell) is a flea. But Orwell parts company with orthodox Soviet criticism when he adds in a sentence immediately following the passage just quoted: 'Not, of course, that Dali's autobiography, or his pictures, ought to be suppressed.'

As a writer any literary man, Orwell believed, had to be a liberal. To be a writer was to belong naturally to the opposition (he found Kipling's identification of himself with the ruling powers, while admitting that it gave his work its grasp of reality, to be both strange and disgusting). Only by being conscious of his political bias could a writer act politically in accordance with necessary group loyalties without sacrificing his integrity. And it may be that the acting and the writing had to be kept in separate compartments, if the writer was to be preserved from any command to misrepresent what Orwell called 'the scenery of his own mind', or even if he was to maintain his imaginative fertility. There is a lengthy passage in one of his last essays, 'Writers and Leviathan' (1948), where Orwell tried to state this rather complex position:

... we should draw a sharper distinction than we do at present between our political and our literary loyalties and should recognize that a willingness to *do* certain distasteful but necessary things does not carry with it any obligation to swallow the beliefs that usually go with them. When a writer engages in politics he should do so as a citizen, as a human being, but not *as a writer*. ... But whatever else he does in the service of his party, he should never write for it. He should make it clear that his writing is a thing apart. And he should be able to act co-operatively while, if he chooses, completely rejecting the official ideology. . . . Sometimes, if a writer is honest, his writings and his political activities may actually contradict one another. There are occasions when that is plainly undesirable; but then the remedy is not to falsify one's impulses, but to remain silent. To suggest that a creative writer, in a time of conflict, must split his life into two compartments, may seem defeatist or frivolous: yet in practice I do not see what else he can do. . . . One half of him which in a sense is the whole of him, can act as resolutely, even as violently if need be, as anyone else. But his writings, in so far as they have any value, will always be the product of the saner self that stands aside, records the things that are done and admits their necessity, but refuses to be deceived as to their true nature.

EYE 24; COL E 432

In 'The Prevention of Literature' (1946) Orwell had written that literature was doomed if liberty of thought perished, whether in a whole society or in an individual. The bought mind was the spoiled mind:

Unless spontaneity enters at some point or another, literary creation is impossible, and language itself becomes ossified. At some time in the future, if the human mind becomes something totally different from what it now is, we may learn to separate literary creation from intellectual honesty. At present we know only that the imagination, like certain wild animals, will not breed in captivity.

SE 132; COL E 324

The free intelligence; a vigorous language; private opinions; the literature of liberalism; the imagination breeding only in freedom; the writer standing aside from whatever activity he may undertake as a citizen, recording, refusing to be deceived— these are the aspects of Orwell's non-fictional hero: the traditional literary intellectual. And like the heroes of the novels, he too was having to swim against the mounting current of his times, for by 1984 literature was going to be produced on the fiction machines and versificators in that home of lies, the Ministry of Truth.

Bibliography

A bibliography of Orwell is being prepared by I. Angus and R. Willison. Much research material is collected in what is known as the Orwell Archive at University College, London.

These are the main publications on Orwell:

- K. Alldritt: *The Making of George Orwell* (Arnold, 1969)
- J. Atkins: *George Orwell* (Calder, 1954)
- L. Brander: *George Orwell* (Longman, 1954)
- J. Calder: *Chronicles of Conscience* (Secker and Warburg, 1969)
- M. Gross (ed.): *The World of George Orwell* (Weidenfeld, 1971)
- C. Hollis: *A Study of George Orwell* (Hollis & Carter, 1956)
- T. Hopkinson: *George Orwell* (Longman PB, 1955)
- R. Rees: *George Orwell—Fugitive from the Camp of Victory* (Secker, 1961)
- P. Stansky and W. Abrahams: *The Unknown Orwell* (Constable, 1972)
- E. M. Thomas: *George Orwell* (Oliver and Boyd PB, 1965)
- R. Williams: *George Orwell* (Fontana PB, 1970)
- G. Woodcock: *The Crystal Spirit: A Study of George Orwell* (Cape, 1967)

These are some books 'on the period'.

- R. Blythe: *The Age of Illusion* (Penguin PB, 1964)
- R. Graves & A. Hodge: *The Long Weekend* (Foursquare PB, 1961)
- J. Laver: *Edwardian Promenade* (Hulton, 1958)
  Between the Wars (Vista Books, 1961)
- C. L. Mowat: *Britain Between the Wars* (University PB, 1968) (especially Chapter 5)
- A. W. Palmer: *A Dictionary of Modern History* (Penguin PB, 1964)
- D. Thomson: *England in the Twentieth Century* (Penguin PB, 1965)

These are more detailed treatments of those aspects of 20th-century history which particularly concerned Orwell:

(a) ENGLAND

C. Cross: *The Fascists in Britain* (Barrie and Rockliff, 1961)

G. Dangerfield: *The Strange Death of Liberal England* (Paladin PB, 1970)

A. Marwick: *The Deluge* (Bodley Head, 1965; Penguin PB, 1967) (especially the first and last chapters)

H. Pelling: *A Short History of the Labour Party* (Macmillan PB, 1966); *The British Communist Party* (Black, 1958)

N. Wood: *Communism and British Intellectuals* (Gollancz, 1959)

(b) RUSSIA

I. Deutscher: *Stalin* (Penguin PB, 1966)

M. Hayward & L. Labedz (eds.): *Literature and Revolution in Soviet Russia* (Oxford, 1963) (especially Chapters 5 and 6)

L. Kochan: *The Making of Modern Russia* (Penguin PB, 1963) (especially the last ten chapters)

L. Schapiro: *The Communist Party of the Soviet Union* (University PB, Methuen, 1963) (especially Chapters 22 and 23)

(c) GERMANY

A. Bullock: *Hitler* (Penguin PB, 1962)

E. Leiser: *A Pictorial History of Nazi Germany* (Penguin PB, 1962)

P. Levi: *If This Is a Man* (Foursquare PB, 1962) (one of the most famous accounts of Auschwitz)

(d) SPAIN

H. D. Ford: *A Poets' War* (Oxford, 1965) (especially the first three chapters)

K. B. Hoskins: *Today the Struggle* (Univ. of Texas, 1969)

R. Payne (ed.): *The Civil War in Spain* (Secker and Warburg, 1963)

H. Thomas: *The Spanish Civil War* (Penguin PB, 1965) (use the index)

K. W. Watkins: *Britain Divided* (Nelson, 1963) (especially Chapter 5)

(e) INDIA

M. Edwardes: *The Last Years of British India* (Cassell, 1963) (especially the first 50 pages)

It may help to put Orwell's various books into perspective if you can relate each one first of all to other books written by him, and also to other books that seem to cover the same territory. This second procedure varies according to your individual literary knowledge: I happen to have read or heard about the books to be mentioned.

1. 'DOWN AND OUT IN PARIS AND LONDON' (1933)

There is a whole literature of vagrancy and destitution: Gorki's play *The Lower Depths*, P. Quennell's selections from Mayhew, *London's Underworld* (Spring Books, 1963) and Jack London's *The People of the Abyss* (Panther PB, 1963) are obvious examples. O'Connor's *Britain in the Sixties: Vagrancy* (Penguin PB, 1963) provides some useful comparative material, and it is interesting to place the atmosphere described in the quotation on p. 16 of the present essay with that of Wesker's play *The Kitchen* (in *New English Dramatists*, vol. 2, Penguin PB, 1960). Orwell's own essay 'How the Poor Die' shows another aspect of his Parisian experience—which can generally be contrasted with that of contemporary American writers (as described, for example, in Hemingway's *A Moveable Feast* (Penguin PB, 1966)). T. Parker's *Unknown Citizen* (Hutchinson, 1963) is a moving account of what can happen to the types described in *Down and Out* even in the Welfare State, as is J. Sandford: *Down and Out in Britain* (New English Library PB, 1971).

2. 'BURMESE DAYS' (1934)

Everyone immediately thinks of Forster's *A Passage to India*. The same writer's *The Hill of Devi* (Penguin PB, 1965) deals with a very different social milieu from Flory's, but there are hints of similar tensions. The second volume of Leonard Woolf's autobiography, *Growing* (Hogarth Press, 1961), describes colonial work in Ceylon just before the First World War. Orwell's own essays 'A Hanging', 'Shooting an Elephant', 'Rudyard Kipling' and 'Marrakech' are related thematically to his novel. Some novels about India by Indian writers are mentioned in the bibliography at the end of R. Segal's *The Crisis of India* (Penguin PB 1965).

3. 'A CLERGYMAN'S DAUGHTER' (1935)

Parts of the novel are obviously related to the English section of *Down and Out*. I find that Butler's *The Way of All Flesh* makes a useful comparison. Gissing's *The Odd Women* (1893) is, like Orwell's novel, a study of middle-class respectability and economic insecurity.

4. 'KEEP THE ASPIDISTRA FLYING' (1936)

Gissing's novel *New Grub Street* (1891) (Oxford, 1958) is about the horrors of a writer's life some thirty or forty years earlier than Comstock's. W. Greenwood's *Love on the Dole* (Penguin, 1969) is about poverty and deals with the same period as Orwell's novel. On money Karl Marx once wrote:

> Money degrades all the gods of man and converts them into commodities. Money is the general and self-constituted value of all things. Consequently it has robbed the whole world—the world of mankind as well as nature—of its peculiar value. Money is the being of man's work and existence alienated from himself, and this alien being rules him, and he prays to it .... contempt for theory, for art, for history, for man as an end in himself, is the real conscious standpoint and virtue of the monied man. The generic relation itself—the relation of man to woman, etc.—becomes an object of commerce.

(The passage, attributed to Marx's *Selected Essays*, is quoted by O'Connor in the book already cited in connection with *Down and Out*. I have been unable to trace the original.)

5. 'THE ROAD TO WIGAN PIER' (1937)

It is worth looking at the statements reprinted in *Human Documents of the Industrial Revolution*, ed. R. Pike (Allen and Unwin, 1966). The classic statement on life in primitive industrial conditions is of course Engels's *The Condition of the Working Class in England* (Allen and Unwin, 1952). J. B. Priestley's *English Journey* (Heinemann, first published in 1934) provides a useful parallel to Orwell's description.

Clancy Sigal's *Weekend in Dinlock* (Penguin PB) describes life in a modern Yorkshire mining community, and contains an account of a visit to the coal face. *Coal is Our Life* (ed. N. Dennis et al., Eyre and Spottiswoode, 1956) is a professional sociological analysis.

6. 'HOMAGE TO CATALONIA' (1938)

Above all this must be read alongside *Animal Farm*. Many of the Englishmen who fought in Spain left accounts of their experiences, but these are now difficult to obtain—a list of them will be found in section 3 of the bibliography to Hugh Thomas's book on the Civil War already cited on p. 139. (Incidentally Thomas says this about Orwell's book: 'His account of the following riots [i.e. the Barcelona street-fighting in May, 1937], marvellously written though it is, is often misleading. It is a better book about war itself than about the Spanish War.') Much of the English poetry written about Spain is quoted in the book by Ford already cited on p. 139.

7. 'COMING UP FOR AIR' (1939)

This often reads as a preliminary study for *Nineteen Eighty-Four*. Gissing's novel *In the Year of the Jubilee* (first published in 1894) is about lower-middle-class life in the London suburbs. Wells's *Mr. Polly* (first published in 1910) describes another retreat from nagging domesticity into a (this time real) country idyll. Many of Bowling's remarks on the wrong course taken by western civilization seem echoes of Mellors' statements in *Lady Chatterley's Lover* (first published in 1928).

8. 'ANIMAL FARM' (1945)

See the notes on *Homage to Catalonia*. There is quite a literature of Communist disillusionment, some examples of which are: R. Crossman (ed.), *The God That Failed* (Bantam Books, 1965); D. Hyde, *I Believed* (World's Work, 1961); M. Djilas, *The New Class* (Unwin PB, 1967). There is a school edition of the book, introduced and annotated by L. Brander, published by Longman.

9. 'NINETEEN EIGHTY-FOUR' (1949)

This book is most obviously related to three other novels: Zamyatin's *We* (Penguin, 1972), Huxley's *Brave New World* (Penguin PB), and Koestler's *Darkness at Noon* (Penguin PB). Further relevant material can be found in J. Strachey: *The Strangled Cry* (Bodley Head, 1962), in W. Sargant: *Battle for the Mind* (Pan PB, 1959) and in C. Milocz: *The Captive Mind* (Mercury PB, Heinemann).

ONE LAST THOUGHT:

Joseph Heller's novel about an American bombing squadron in Italy, *Catch-22* (Corgi PB), contains a conversation between an old Italian woman and the novel's central figure Yossarian —a bomb-aimer who has lost his nerve, and who is only concerned to escape from the activities of an organization which seems bent on destroying him. She defines for him the 'catch' which gives the book its title when she describes how the military police have smashed up the apartment where the flying officers kept their girls:

> 'There must have been a reason,' Yossarian persisted, pounding his fist into his hand. 'They couldn't just barge in here and chase everyone out.'
>
> 'No reason,' wailed the old woman. 'No reason.'
>
> 'What right did they have?'
>
> 'Catch-22.'
>
> '*What?*' Yossarian froze in his tracks in fear and alarm and felt his whole body begin to tingle. '*What* did you say?'
>
> 'Catch-22,' the old woman repeated, rocking her head up and down. 'Catch-22. Catch-22 says they have a right to do anything we can't stop them from doing.'

Index